SALSA CHICA

SALSA CHICA

HOW I LEARNED TO DANCE SALSA AND AVOID REAL LIFE

SOLANGE CASTRO

© 2020 by Solange Castro

All rights reserved. This book or any portion thereof may not be reproduced or used in any manner whatsoever without the express written permission of the publisher except for the use of brief quotations in a book review.

ISBN: 9781790486366 (paperback)

For my mother, Rafie

Dancing with Charlie at the Warehouse, 2009
photo credit: Kevin Hahn

Table of Contents

Introduction ix

Chapter 1	Casa Escobar 1
Chapter 2	Wax On, Wax Off 13
Chapter 3	Dress Salsa 27
Chapter 4	A World of Boyfriends 35
Chapter 5	The Relentless Salsero 49
Chapter 6	What a Feeling! 59
Chapter 7	Childless Spinster 71
Chapter 8	Jazzy Mambo 79
Chapter 9	Leopard Print Grandma 87
Chapter 10	Marriage vs. Salsa 93
Chapter 11	Salsa Abroad 107
Chapter 12	La Palabra (The Word) 117
Chapter 13	Salsa Boundaries 125
Chapter 14	Todo Tiene Su Final (Everything Comes to an End) 133
Chapter 15	Forever Salsa Chica 143

Acknowledgments 151
About the Author 153
Bibliography 155

Introduction

Prior to the time covered in this book, "dance salsa" appeared on my endless, somewhat masochistic to-do list, lodged between "buy container for rice," and "birth child." Once I learned to dance salsa, I did little else. I worked and I danced. Try as I might, I could not imagine a more desirable way to spend my free time. I became a "salsa addict," "*salsera*," or "salsa chica," a woman who rearranges her entire life to accommodate her need to dance as much as humanly possible.

It was a big experiment at first. What would happen if I went out and danced night after night? Would my body fall apart? (No.) Would I be able to function at work? (Sometimes.) Would my mom get mad at me? (Yes.)

I simply got tired and slept through the night. I also lost weight and toned my arms and legs without forcing myself to get on a hamster-wheel torture device surrounded by people who refuse to make eye contact. I grew more comfortable in my own skin and developed confidence and a new appreciation for my body, even my feet with their long, fingerlike toes. I no longer believed that I lacked anything: a child, a husband, a house, or cool boots. I felt grateful for my life.

I once told a first date that I danced salsa and he replied, "Sounds vapid." I defended the lifestyle and then spent the next few years wondering if he was right. Was my single lifestyle shallow? Were people in marriages deeper people? My mother thought so. While other people procreated, I danced.

How does one become a salsa dancer? This book, which grew out of my blog, is a memoir-ish account of the literal and figurative steps I took to learn to dance and make my own choices in life. I changed names and identifying characteristics and took some creative license.

Did I avoid real life? It depends on how you look at it. I never did birth a child or buy a rice container. But dance? That I crossed off the list. I do not regret any of it.

Chapter 1
Casa Escobar

Step 1: Get out of the car.

When you do dance, I wish you
A wave o' th' sea, that you might ever do
Nothing but that.
   —Shakespeare, *The Winter's Tale*

Dancers in salsa shoes, 2009

SOLANGE CASTRO

The girl danced like she owned her body. Not just her body, but her red dress, dance partner, the floor, and everyone who stood around and watched her, including me. She looked to something inside herself, or the music—I could not really tell.

It took me less than five minutes to drive to Casa Escobar, a Mexican restaurant located a mile from my house. Then I stayed in my car for an hour.

Just open the door, I thought, as I sat in my red Honda Civic.

Mascara-infused tears flowed down my face. Single. Alone. Out by myself on a Sunday night. While only thirty-four, I felt like a character from a Tennessee Williams play, past my prime and rife with desperation.

I could go home and watch *Sex and the City*. Or work on my OkCupid profile, I thought. Sure, I had those options. But I always had those options. I needed to move forward and, if not forward, then sideways. I needed to, at the very least, get out of the car.

I opened my car door and walked inside Casa Escobar, where I met the great love of my life: salsa.

Casa Escobar, a dive-y Mexican restaurant located five blocks from my apartment in Marina Del Rey, California, hosted a salsa night each Sunday on their small, tile dance floor. I paid fifteen dollars for the class taught by an Argentinean instructor and spent the hour flooded with different emotions: shame, fear, embarrassment, and a short fleeting moment of joy. My body on display for the world to witness. What was the next step? Stripping? After the class ended, the DJ played salsa music, and I danced with my classmates, all men, most of whom repeated the choreography they had just learned.

After a while I noticed the arrival of dancers who all seemed to know each other. One young Latino man with large biceps and spiked, bleached-blond hair greeted everyone and then danced with the girl in the red dress.

I stopped dancing and watched Spiked Blond Hair and Red Dress Girl. Halfway through the song, Spiked Blond Hair signaled to another young Latino man in a jacket with the name "Guanajuato" stitched on the back. Guanajuato stepped in and took Spiked Blond Hair's place as leader. Meanwhile, Spiked Blond Hair took a swig of his Corona. Guanajuato looked a little drunk, but Red Dress Girl did not notice. She looked fantastic.

"They are gorgeous," said the woman beside me. I turned to find a tall, white woman in her forties. She poured clear liquid from a flask into a glass of soda water and then put the flask back into her purse.

"It's organic, wheat-free vodka. They don't serve it here," she explained. "It helps me feel more free."

She introduced herself as Lisa and we, along with a growing crowd, continued to watch Spiked Blond Hair and Guanajuato dance with Red Dress Girl. We looked like fans entranced by stars on the red carpet.

"I can't believe it…salsa," said Lisa. Except she pronounced it with a thick gringo accent, which made the word sound like "saul-sa." "This…" She waved at the dance floor. "It's all I want to do with my life. It would be one thing if I were in my thirties, but at my age? I'm going to be fifty!"

I felt an instant kinship with Lisa. Like her, I wanted to dance. More than anything.

"Have you danced with that guy?" she asked and pointed to a tall, lanky Latino man who stood by the DJ. He played what looked like a percussive instrument to the music. A far-shorter Latino guy stood beside him with an instrument that sounded like a jar full of beads. I later learned that they were following the "clave," the fundamental beat in salsa.

"No," I said. I felt a little rejected. Why had he not asked me to dance?

"He picked me up and threw me in the air," she said with indignation. "I could have died!"

I looked at my watch and saw that it was almost midnight. It felt scandalous to be out so late on a work night. Do these people have jobs?

"I have to go home," I said and made my exit. Nobody but Lisa noticed. But I felt a pull to stay.

I came home filled with fresh hope. A wall of fear lay crumpled behind me, along with my knee length skirt.

I went back to Casa Escobar the next Sunday. And the Sunday after that. Each week I saw Lisa, Spiked Blond Hair, Guanajuato, Red Dress Girl, and a host of other people who also scheduled their lives around Casa Escobar's salsa night. Casa Escobar transformed my

SALSA CHICA

Sunday nights from existential loneliness to something akin to a religious experience.

In time, I danced with everyone, including the guys who played instruments beside the DJ. Indeed, when I danced with the tall one, named Milo, he picked me up and threw me in the air, just like Lisa said. When I danced with the shorter one, named Santiago, he stopped dead cold for a beat and stared at my feet. Then he fanned his face as if I was setting him ablaze with my sexy style. He looked at Milo, who stood nearby, and pointed to my feet, as if they were on fire. His shtick seemed a little exaggerated, as I clearly had no idea what I was doing during my "dance solo." But he made me feel special and honored throughout the whole dance, even when he pulled me close and I felt him grind against my thigh. (Please note: "grinding" is not a part of salsa dancing.)

In time, I realized that I, in fact, had no style. I needed some moves and so, a few weeks later, I signed up for a "Ladies' Styling" workshop taught by the same Argentinean instructor. At the class I saw Lisa, who waved at me. The teacher taught us movements, like how to execute a "butt roll." Lisa later told me that she felt ripped off by what she described as the teacher's "stripper moves."

Nonetheless, I signed up for more classes. One night, in another class, the straps of my Nine West spiked-heel sandals broke, and the teacher offered me her extra pair of salsa shoes. The suede bottoms allowed me to glide, the straps provided my ankles with support, and the soles melted around my feet. I fell in love.

The next day I looked up the website for the store. The home page featured three couples in dramatic poses. The women wore tight buns and fierce facial expressions, as if they could not contain the emotion of The Dance. The men were clad in what looked like *Star Trek* uniforms. Lightning bolts flashed in the background. The whole site, which looked like it was built in 1996, seemed like a *Saturday Night Live* parody of salsa. But that only made me love salsa more. As I would soon learn, there is no irony in salsa dancing. The writer in me balked at the vulnerability. Unlike the ironic detachment that I embraced in my blog posts, hammered out in my free time at my job at a digital ad agency, dancing comes from real emotion.

I drove to Van Nuys and purchased my first pair of salsa shoes. I danced in them until the shoe repairman could no longer reconstruct the bottoms. Then I bought another pair of the same shoe, and then another. Years later I have worn out over a dozen shoes: bored holes in the soles, shredded the straps, and annihilated the linings. However, the heels often remain intact because I dance on the balls of my feet.

The first night I wore my shoes at Casa Escobar, I looked down on the newbies in their stilettos. What amateurs. I was official, a real salsa dancer. In time, Lisa bought the same shoes. The moment we put on our shoes, hunched over in our chairs, we switched over from civilian life and into our salsa personas. While I showed up at work with a desperate need for caffeine and a brush, the moment I stepped out onto the dance floor with my salsa shoes, I felt flooded with goddess energy.

Lisa and I quickly realized that we needed our dance partners as much as the music, and we scrutinized them with intense curiosity.

One night, Lisa ran up to me, as if she'd heard some earth-shattering news.

"You're not going to believe this, but Milo is Santiago's father!"

"That's so *Chinatown*," I replied.

Lisa discovered this one night at an after-Casa Escobar party located at what she described as the "compound" where Santiago, Milo, and Guanajuato and his younger brother all lived. All of them migrated from Mexico and fell into a category of salsa dancer that we came to know as a "salsero."

What is a salsero? In the nonverbal culture of salsa, the definition remained fluid. A salsero could be a man who loved salsa music, dancing, and a personal style that thrived in the Los Angeles (LA) salsa scene from the late 90s to the 00s. Picture fedoras, three-piece suits, chains, and, yes, even sunglasses at night. A woman with the same passion and drive to dance became a "salsera." Her style, though less distinct, included tight dresses, but mostly jeans and a tight-fitted top.

Salseros and salseras followed the culture of LA Style

Salsa, established in the nineties by the three Vasquez brothers—Johnny, Francisco, and Luis—and the wife of Johnny, Joby Brava. All belonged to "Salsa Brava," a dance group that cross-pollinated salsa all over the world. LA Style Salsa had a reputation for showy, flashy moves and big tricks. In Los Angeles clubs, salseros vied for attention with crowd-pleasers like dips and something called the "neck drop"—where a woman's head hovers inches from the floor—which most salsa clubs outlaw today, thank God.

We were hardly salsa dancers, let alone salseras. We still held a "beginner" status that made us fresh meat for the mostly regular crowd of male dance partners. When we weren't dancing, Lisa, her friend Amy, and I stood around and discussed our dances. Nicknames were paramount for survival in salsa. It's not unusual for salsa dancers to dance with each other for years and fail to grasp a name. In the absence of this information, identifying a dancer can resemble a Native American naming ritual. We often referred to dancers by the way they danced, what they wore, or who they dated.

"Short Hat Guy"

"Blond Girl Who Dances with Guy with Braces"

"Persian Hat Guy"

"Smells Like Mildew"

Lisa's friend, Amy, came up with nicknames for everyone and dubbed Blond Spiked Hair and Guanajuato, "The Ninjas." Lisa and Amy discussed the Ninjas with starry eyes and deep sighs, like teenagers, and deemed them the greatest dancers at Casa Escobar, if not Los Angeles.

The first time Spiked Blond Hair asked me to dance, I felt like a freshman asked to prom by the captain of the football team. Lisa later told me that when she saw Spiked Blond Hair approach me with his hand extended, she turned to Amy and announced, "Solange has arrived."

That night I learned Spiked Blond Hair's real name, Ruben, and that he worked as a valet at a high-end Beverly Hills restaurant. He clearly had no shortage of dance partners. Indeed, Ruben's steady stream of partners (girlfriends?) and King of Casa Escobar status seemed to prove the age-old adage, women love a man who can dance.

In time, I came to see that the Casa Escobar Ninjas were more performers, or "show-offs," as one partner stated with an eye roll, than models of technical style. At any given time, Ruben, Guanajuato—also known as Juan—and his brother, who they called *"Suavecito"* (The Smooth One) might embark on an impromptu salsa show involving flips and a willing salsera in the ubiquitous tradition wherein dancers trade off dancing with the same girl. Each guy shows off his best moves for eight counts, takes a break, has a swig of his Corona, and lets the girl sweat out the song. Lisa called it the "Salsa Gang Bang" once, and while I am reticent to apply a rape analogy to a dance I adore, it does speak to the gross male privilege that pervades the culture of salsa (and the world).

However, the tradition also honored the skill and power of the salsera. Many amazing powerful salseras, like Red Dress Girl, participated in and even enjoyed the challenge, including, for a short time, myself.

I was a beginner at Casa Escobar. This meant that I chose partners without discrimination. I said, "Yes," to everyone. Never is a person so open to people from all walks of life as those infused with a passion to learn a new partner dance. I danced with older, lonely men, quirky guys who gyrated or circled me. I tolerated a lot of weirdness because I had no idea what I was doing. In those days, it all looked like "salsa dancing" to me.

For my first few years, neither was I skilled enough, nor did I possess the consciousness of the music to keep up at the high-profile venues, like Steven's Steakhouse, where "the real dancers went," according to the seasoned pros who entered Casa Escobar with swagger.

A few dancers introduced me to outdoor salsa on Santa Monica's Third Street Promenade, an open-air shopping mall near the ocean, on Sunday afternoons. Soon I spent my Sundays at two different venues. I danced through the late afternoon on the "promenade" where a DJ set up a boom box in front of tourists and families. Stray toddlers often wandered into the fray, drawn by the music, and we did our best not to step on them. Afterward, I straggled into Casa Escobar like a wedding guest who refuses to leave the reception.

Casa Escobar people weren't amazing salsa dancers or exceptionally salsa-y—not a lot of three-piece suits and sunglasses made it to the tile dance floor. They ran the gamut of ages, races, and income levels: young teenagers, who couldn't get into over-twenty-one clubs, and over-fifty men, who preferred the slower songs. Not swanky or hip, Casa Escobar was one thing that all salsa dancers love, and that is free.

In the grand universe of Salsa World in 2006, Casa Escobar was a tiny moon or a piece of stray asteroid rock. However, it was the perfect place to start learning how to dance salsa on a Sunday night.

The cast of Casa Escobar characters included more people than I could possibly fit into one book: Ernie, a fifty-something rotund man, who could tell you just how long everyone had been dancing; Luis, a 5'2" man in a hat, who someone once described as "The Jumping Bean" because he jumped so much while dancing (I always thought it was so he could reach the height of his partner); Alonzo, a man we sometimes referred to as "Al Capone," who would disappear for months to, as rumor had it, serve time; Marty, a fifty-something woman, who had a reputation for trading sex in exchange for free admission to clubs; and Raul, a clean-cut forty-something guy, who looked like an investment banker and whom I later deemed Relentless for his style of courtship (if you can call it that).

The music of salsa brought together this diverse group of people into a happy state of collegial joy and seemed to bridge race, class, age, and even language stratification. The fifty-five-year-old white, Jewish accountant and the twenty-one-year-old Mexican baggage claim worker shared only a few moves and love for salsa music. But that proved enough.

In those first few months, I sometimes watched a young Latino guy with a ponytail, worn under a red bandana and a fedora. He and a broad-shouldered young man in a baseball cap stood near the door and watched the scene like security guards.

In those early days of Casa Escobar, salsa felt like an alternative universe, where souls came out of their ascribed identities of gardener, accountant, waiter, wife or husband, and father or mother. A friend once remarked that in Salsa World people created real-life avatars. Women of any age, shape, or size became beautiful and every man held the cache of rock stars. Salsa seemed to have the power to transform the most jaded, like Lisa, or the shyest and most confused women, like me.

Chapter 2
Wax On, Wax Off

Step 2: Meet your salsa guru.

Hard times require furious dancing.
—Alice Walker

Dancers at Mor Bar in Santa Monica, 2006,
photo credit: Kevin Hahn

One night I danced with a tall man of Middle Eastern descent.

"You're too strong," he said.

"Too much power yoga," I replied.

"You're not letting me lead," he said, a note of frustration in his voice. "American women. They can't follow."

I refused to dance with him again, but he had a point. Lack of equality is a great organizing principal. Partner dancing requires one leader, and one follower. But I followed as well as a three-year-old and dancers took notice. If I wanted good dancers to ask me to dance, I had to improve my following skills. I have since learned to follow and to lead. I prefer following. Followers develop great reflexes, intelligence, and a certain freedom. However, in order to become a great follower, I had to give up something that I really enjoyed: control.

The Argentinean teacher emphasized in class that salsa dancing was "the last place in America where men are *in charge*." Well, in entertainment, technology, medicine, and every high-paying field. But, yes, in those days, in salsa, too.

I thought I was a born follower. I had followed boyfriends into all kinds of terrible experiences: long afternoons at sports bars, hikes in the pouring rain, and bad sex. A boyfriend once took me to look at an apartment located under the LAX flight path.

But a leech isn't following anybody; it's attached. No, a follower does not adhere to the leader, just as a leader does not control his partner. A follower responds to the leader, and both serve the highest calling, the music, which I decided comes from divine providence. Following, I concluded, after months of struggle with a multitude of partners, is an act of faith.

But I needed more than just following skills. After my initial Fresh Meat status at Casa Escobar dissipated, the Good Dancers, the real salseros, hardly clamored to dance with me. I had not shown enough interest in them sexually, and I did not have the skill to make the dance worth their time. I could see the difference when a real salsera walked into the club, like Red Dress Girl. She knew what she was doing. She strutted in, utterly disinterested in the men or anything other than the act of expressing herself through salsa. She saw beyond a salsa dance, looked down from the heavens, and moved the chess pieces of her life. Lisa and I studied the moves of Red Dress Girl. I later introduced myself to her like the awkward outcast who meets the head cheerleader.

I could hardly hear the beat, let alone dance to it. I frequently spun out of control, but I wanted to learn flashy choreography to show off during my solos. I failed to realize that the course of my salsa education stretched out before me like a long, rocky Himalayan road.

One day I saw the young man in the ponytail and fedora eye me, and so I made the bold choice to approach him. He seemed unsurprised by my interest in him and introduced himself as "Angel."

"I've seen you around," he said.

"Yes, I've seen you, too."

We exchanged vital statistics, and I learned that he worked for the United States Postal Service.

"How long have you been dancing?" I asked.

"Well, it depends. Seven years, if you count the time before I was 'educated.'"

"What do you mean by 'educated'?"

"Before I understood salsa music."

His tone seemed to give the word "salsa" a reverence. It was almost like he said "money" or "God."

"I can help you out, if you want."

"What do you mean?"

"I can give you a lesson."

"Really? How much do you charge?"

"Don't worry about it, White Girl," he ended.

He didn't seem like a serial killer and, to be honest, I was intrigued. He had style and a sort of irreverent charisma. Mostly, however, my desire to improve bordered on desperation. I felt tired of the awkward intermediate phase, scrounging around for partners with decent hygiene and a smooth lead. If only the Good Dancers asked me to dance, wanted to dance with me. Maybe Angel could teach me something, I thought. So—crazy as it now seems—I invited this intense young man into my apartment for a "private lesson."

Such an arrangement, I later learned, arose with regularity in Salsa World. A female beginner found a salsero more than happy to "teach" her. Such pairings, formed

SALSA CHICA

by ulterior motives, progressed or ended to the degree that underlying desires—sex and/or salsa instruction—found fulfillment.

"You got a pretty nice place here, White Girl," said Angel upon entering my apartment.

We moved my coffee table and rug aside and then stood in the middle of my apartment.

"I've been watching you," he said. He pointed his peace sign fingers to his eyes and then to me. "You sway your hips during the cross-body lead."

He imitated my steps, crossing each foot, slightly pigeon-toed, with an exaggerated hip motion.

"I don't dance like that."

"Yes, you do. 'White girls' try to insert an extra move into their salsa," he explained. "They dance their *idea of salsa*."

"Well, I'm not actually white…I happen to be half Mexican."

"So, you're a half-white girl?"

"Sure, I guess."

"OK then, Half-White Girl…think of the cross-body lead as a walk," he continued. "The flavor will come."

Flavor? Like pistachio or smoky barbecue? But I didn't say anything. He spoke with so much sincerity.

"What kind of music do you have?"

"I have some Marc Anthony…"

He laughed as if I had said something funny.

"Forget the music. We'll start without it."

SOLANGE CASTRO

We got into the basic "closed position."

"Stand up straight," he said. "Hold your head high and stick your chest out…as if…" He searched for the right words. "As if you're a conceited, stuck-up Beverly Hills bitch."

I stood up straight but kept my chest level with my shoulders. I didn't want him looking at my boobs. I felt uncomfortable under this 25-year-old's tutelage, and, yet, I trusted him. He clearly believed in the sanctity of salsa.

We practiced the "basic step" and he made me count each step. I was used to counting from classes. For months, maybe years, I counted each step—1, 2, 3…5, 6, 7—to every song.

"Practice your moves every night slowly, and then gradually do them to music."

Practice moves? I thought dancers developed skills by showing up on the dance floor. I could not imagine Ruben or Guanajuato practicing at home.

After the lesson I walked Angel to his car.

"Can I ask you a question?" he asked.

"Shoot," I replied. I knew what was coming.

"Would you ever consider a younger guy?" he asked.

"Sure," I replied. I could tell the possibility seemed necessary for the arrangement to continue. By that point I believed that Angel could lead me to a new level of salsa and myself.

After that night Angel appointed himself my Mr. Miyagi. He became my first Salsa Guru. He would probably be my Patrick Swayze or John Travolta, the male lead in the dance movie of my life, if I had shown an iota of interest. But whatever his expectations were that we might develop some "cougar" relationship, all he got was the unsolicited advice of an older half-white girl.

I felt comfortable with him and in salsa, in part, from a childhood spent growing up in a Latino community in Berkeley, California. I grew up shopping at Kmart with my single mom, but unlike Angel, both my parents had gone to college.

"Stop telling me that I'm smart and should go to college all the time," he said one night.

I stopped playing counselor and just listened to his opinions and thoughts about salsa and American culture. Which is all he wanted from me. I had many teachers in salsa, but Angel articulated the spirit of salsa in a way that I never forgot.

"I've noticed that when guys first start dancing, it's all about meeting girls," he told me one night.

We stood outside of Mor Bar, a bowling alley–shaped bar on Main Street in Santa Monica with a shoe-destroying cement floor and the ventilation system of a coal mine.

"But gradually, it becomes about dancing," he continued. "It's just something that I've noticed," he added, more to himself. Despite a wiry frame and youthful face, he carried himself with the stoic detachment of an eighty-year-old on a porch swing.

Salsa structured Angel's perception of manhood in all its permutations. It shaped his worldview, from fedoras to white girls to respect for his body. Salsa gave him an identity, separate from his family or the US Postal Service.

He liked to hold court in front of a captive audience and found new dancers to listen to his endless waxing of salsa wisdom.

"Salsa means mixture," he explained one night to a group outside of Mor Bar. "Afro-Cuban, tango and ballroom all combined. It's really a street dance."

The Mor Bar Salsa Night fell on a Monday, which rendered me exhausted by Tuesday. I recovered enough to attend Wednesday salsa at Monsoon, a famous club in Santa Monica. But by Friday I fell asleep on my couch around eight o'clock.

Angel told me that he lived with his parents and was one of eight children—all girls, except him. He lived in East LA but drove out to the Westside because of the higher density of white girls.

"I love white girls," he told me one night over dinner at a Cuban restaurant in Culver City.

"I've noticed," I replied. I had yet to see a blond girl enter the club who did not end up as his partner for at least a few songs, if not longer.

"I think you have internalized American racism," I offered.

"What?"

"You value white skin."

"I just think blue eyes are more beautiful. Everyone thinks that. Ask anyone."

SALSA CHICA

My social justice lesson fell on deaf ears.

"I like white girls because they are vulnerable," he continued. "I want to go to Sweden and get me a blond and blue-eyed girl. When I bring her back here, I'm not letting her out of the house."

Such statements left me dubious about the future of our friendship. While I saw a charismatic, bright young man, I could not dismiss his misogyny as ironic shock material, such as that used by terrible stand-up comics. He believed his words. But Angel was hardly the only Latino male with an attraction to white girls. Salsa World often seemed like The Forbidden Love Zone of Los Angeles, the battleground where the Latino male wreaked vengeance on the white male power structure. The indignities of service jobs, racism, and police harassment met justice in the least violent place in America: the dance floor.

I watched the following scene play out several times: a white guy—affluent, attractive, college-educated—stands alone by the bar all night, sipping his Amstel Light and staring in disbelief while his girlfriend dances with a short, dark-skinned man, who may or may not have a job in the service industry and/or a need for a Green Card. The dancer might be handsome, built, and tall. Or he might be in need of some dental work. Regardless of his physical appearance, women of various backgrounds, transfixed by the music, possibly possessed by some kind of Latino fever, and mesmerized by his ability to move to a rhythm will forego traditional upper-middle-class standards around education and income for a good lead. Or what they understand to be a good lead. There's no arguing the facts: women love a man who can dance.

Angel cherished the VIP passport to a woman's body that his salsa skills granted him. And with the constant flow of women who wandered into clubs with a "what is salsa?" curiosity, he never lacked for new opportunities to impress, attract, and seduce women of all skin colors, but mostly white. And if he didn't succeed in consummating the relationship, he rested assured that said girl would never find a dancer better than him. Sure, he worked for the postal service, but he felt himself to be a rich man.

Despite his provocations and overall pain-in-the-ass personality, I tolerated and followed Angel's "wax on, wax off" instructions. Whatever misguided ideas he had about white girls, he did know more about salsa than I did.

"If you really want to dance salsa you can't be a 'soul dancer,'" he lectured me one night. "It's not about the feeling that you get from the song or the alcohol or your partner. You're not a 'party dancer.' You're a dancer. A servant to the music."

The idea that my dancing "served the music" sounded pretentious to me, but I figured such aphorisms made him feel superior. A feeling he clearly enjoyed.

"And if you want to dance *bad ass* you dance 'On 2.'"

I had heard of people who danced "On 2," but it would be a few years before I attempted to learn it.

SALSA CHICA

While a well-known figure in the community, Angel wasn't exactly popular. He told one friend that her salsa "had no point" and another that she danced an "imitation of salsa." He openly expressed dislike for other dancers, declined dance offers with impunity, and gossiped about the scandalous relationships of salseras. One comment on a YouTube video of him described him as "*El Sucio*"—"The Dirty One."

But the opinion of other people mattered little to Angel. His life consisted of salsa, his job, and women, in that order. He introduced me to a new kind of guy, a heterosexual man who loves dancing beyond anything else.

Perhaps because I felt some truth in his words, I invited his feedback.

"Your salsa needs to be angrier and more aggressive," he told me one night. "And don't smile," he added. "Don't get happy when you dance."

"But what if I'm having fun?"

"For now, have an expression on your face, as if you're in the 'militry.'"

"The what?"

"The military. I call it 'militry' because it sounds better."

On the point of not smiling, I came to agree with him. (I also agreed with his pronunciation of "militry.") Looking too happy falls in the same category as the sexy face, which plagues many dancers. I began to understand that a dancer who "serves the music" dignifies the art form with stoicism. I had thought that if I smiled and "looked happy" a partner would ask me to dance again. As a result, my salsa reeked of a little girl's need to manipulate the world in order to get what she wants. I wanted to become a mature dancer who interprets the music through her body. However, there is also the whole idea of "having fun," which came much later.

However, "feeling the music" required a sense of the music that I had yet to acquire. I wanted to tear out onto the dance floor like I did in seventh grade to Prince's "Let's Go Crazy."

"Your problem is that you have no patience," he said to me one night. We stood in the middle of the dance floor while he stared at me with obvious distaste.

"You need to listen to the music. Don't rush."

I did not disagree. But I did tire of his constant criticism and preoccupation with my subpar salsa skills.

One December morning, almost a year after we met, Angel called me at eight o'clock. I had been laid off from my job at the digital advertising agency the day before Thanksgiving. I planned to dance every night until I found another job.

"I've been thinking about your level of salsa," he started.

"My level of salsa?" I asked.

"I'm just not sure if you have 'the fire,'" he said.

"The what…"

"The fire."

"What is 'the fire'?"

SALSA CHICA

"I just don't think you have it in you." He neglected to explain.

"Maybe I don't," I responded. "But it's just salsa."

"Just salsa?"

I got off the phone.

Angel taught me a lot. But "the fire," however, was not something anyone could teach me. I would have to find that myself.

Chapter 3
Dress Salsa

Step 3: Shop for salsa clothes.

It's always the badly dressed people who are the most interesting.

—Jean Paul Gaultier

Posing with my dance team partner, 2007

"If you want to dance hip-hop, you have to dress hip-hop," Angel said to me one night. "If you want to dance salsa, you dress salsa."

We stood by the bar at Monsoon, the seminal Westside salsa club in Santa Monica. Monsoon hosted a salsa band every Wednesday and Saturday night for years in the late 00s. While we waited, the band set up. The leader, Johnny Polanco, a Tony Soprano-look-alike saxophone player, led a large orchestra whose brass section could be heard from the parking lot. In those years, Monsoon hosted every major LA salsa band including Son Mayor, Chino Espinoza y Los Dueños Del Son, Salsa Caliente, and the Susie Hansen Latin Band, led by an American violinist, whom Lisa referred to as "that white chick." Despite the cavelike acoustics of the cavernous room, people came from all over LA to dance till two o'clock.

On this particular night the crowd consisted of non-salsa people, basic civilians who wanted to unwind from the week, and a few scattered dancers. Angel described the scene as "some lame ass shit."

"Don't take this the wrong way," he added. "But you dress like a grandma."

I don't think he ever said "don't take this the wrong way." He never spared my feelings.

I looked down at my floral, knee-length skirt and button-down top. My style could be described as Marshalls meets librarian. Not quite a "grandma," but I showed very little skin. I later put it in a bag for Goodwill.

"He just wants to see you in less clothes," said Lisa.

A few weeks after the "grandma" comment, I went shopping to find clothes that might look more "salsa." What are "salsa clothes"? Lisa described them as "something you wouldn't be caught dead in at work."

"Do you think the over-thirty-five salsa fashion police are going to come after me if I wear this?" I asked Lisa as I walked out of the dressing room in a miniskirt.

"There's no fashion police in salsa," she replied.

I looked at the price on the skirt and decided that fifty dollars was more than I was willing to pay.

Salsa Clothes Rule 1: Spend as little as possible. Salsa clothes absorb sweat (your own as well as that of your partners), and the hand grime of guys who may or may not wash their hands after going to the bathroom.

For a good year, shopping for salsa clothes became an obsession. When I wasn't working or dancing, I combed malls, boutiques, and thrift stores. However, after many wardrobe malfunctions, I realized that most adorable dresses and tops were not made for dancing. Thin fabric ripped and flowy lace got caught in shoes.

"You can wear what you want, but I'm telling you that the best outfit for a salsera is jeans and a tight top and a tight belt," said Angel.

Just by observation I could see that he was right. Great salseras danced in tight-fitting clothes that allowed them to execute body isolations.

Salsa Clothes Rule 2: Dance in clothes that allow you to move.

I found a Latin dance website and purchased a spandex miniskirt, which I wore with a fitted top. I purchased some long, Lycra boy shorts so I wouldn't flash the world while I spun. I now had a dancing uniform.

"Why do you wear those biker shorts?" asked Angel one night at Casa Escobar.

"They are called boy shorts."

They did look like biker shorts, though.

The truth is less fabric worked for me on a glandular level. In the first years, I lost ten pounds in mere water weight. I came home after a night of dancing and peeled off soaked clothes.

One night after a long night of dancing at Monsoon I drove to the 7-Eleven for my post-dancing Gatorade fix with a friend.

"You bin in the pool?" asked the guy behind the counter. The air conditioner at Monsoon died, and, as a result, I looked like someone had thrown me in the hot tub at a bachelorette party.

As I became a better dancer, my body changed, my muscles performed movements with efficiency, and I no longer looked like I'd jumped into a pool. I like to think that I sweated out my old self. Pain, trauma, guilt, and shame broke out of my molecules in nights of drenched sweat, and my real self emerged in body and soul.

So, in addition to my skirts getting shorter, my jeans got tighter. I started to show more of my body. I always thought that the more body shape I showed, the more provocative I might feel. But the opposite happened.

SALSA CHICA

I felt more natural, and down-to-earth. I didn't hide my stomach or butt. I just let it all be what it is.

Salsa proved the safest community for unconventional body types in Los Angeles. I watched pear-shaped women with notable stomachs look far more relaxed than any of the hard-bodied Lululemon-swathed yoga girls.

My legs became two strong sticks, my arms toned up, and before I knew it strangers asked, "Are you doing Pilates?"

I was the last to notice. Salsa dancing gave me the strongest and most fit body I ever inhabited without it ever being a conscious goal. Salsa also gave me the aerobic stamina of an athlete. One day, I went to the doctor to get a skin growth examined, and he insisted I get an EKG because my heart beat only thirty-six times a minute. Low blood pressure runs in my family, but one salsa dance is like a three-minute sprint. "Your heart will live forever," said the doctor. "You should consider donating it." I left humming the tune to "My Heart Will Go On" from *Titanic*.

However, the more I grew as a dancer and focused on the skill and technique of salsa, the less I cared about what I looked like. My hair and makeup faced imminent destruction after one song, and I gave up efforts to control it. Besides the last thing I wanted was a drunk guy to approach me because of my sparkly dress and cat eyes. On some nights, when I really wanted to lose myself in the music, I wore little or no makeup. Sometimes I looked flat-out bad. I just wanted to dance.

SOLANGE CASTRO

Angel recommended that I study with other teachers. So I joined World Champion Christian Oviedo's dance team and then Joby Brava's Ladies' Styling Team. Unknown to laypeople, each of these dancers proved a force in salsa dancing in the late 90s and early 00s, a time when teachers and performers held movie star status in salsa clubs.

Joby first broke down the "body roll," a belly-dance move that consists of a literal roll from your chest to your hips, into miniscule movements. I spent months working on my body roll. Whenever I felt down at work, I went into the bathroom and performed a mini body-roll in front of the mirror. Afterward, I returned to my desk, reconnected to my body and feeling human again.

Joby and Christian challenged my ability to style, spin, and wear sparkly costumes and false eyelashes. I did not love the accoutrements of LA Style but said "yes" to any direction given by an authority figure in salsa. I drove on freeways I had never heard of to take workshops and paid hundreds of dollars to attend salsa congresses (for some reason they are called "congresses" though no laws are passed). I hosted salsa-style workshops in my apartment for Lisa and friends. My passion for salsa structured my life and free time. I didn't know why, but I knew I had to master my moves. Why do people climb Mount Everest? Why bake when you can buy a pie?

Studying with Joby, Christian, and others allowed me to bust out of the awkward intermediate phase. I became a salsera.

SALSA CHICA

And then one day, Angel refused to dance with me. He neglected to inform me how I had offended him, but I assumed that my tolerance of his personality no longer sufficed as payment for his interest in my level of salsa. One night a few months later he caught my eye across the dance floor and gave me an approving thumbs up. We were friends again. And then we had a falling out. Then we were friends again. This went on for years until one day we settled on the occasional nod.

At that point, he had nothing else to teach me. And so we both continued down our paths, deeper into our dance and ourselves.

Chapter 4
A World of Boyfriends

Step 4: Date a salsero.

Dancing begets warmth, which is the parent of wantonness. It is, Sir, the great grandfather of cuckoldom.

—Henry Fielding

Dancers at Mor Bar in Santa Monica, 2006, photo credit: Kevin Hahn

"If you want to get married, Chica, you gotta find a husband now," warned Lisa one night. She called me "Chica," and, in time, she referred to every woman in salsa as a "Salsa Chica." "Because it gets a lot harder when you're my age."

Lisa seemed forever dejected by her single status. And yet, she spent all her free time dancing with men she would hardly consider suitable prospects.

"I don't feel like dating or looking for a husband," I responded. "I just want to dance."

"Well, marriage is security for when you're older and not cute anymore."

While her explanation struck me as a terrible reason to get married, I nodded somberly. I understood. I may not have wanted a family but like most healthy humans, I did seek love.

There is no model in our culture for that in-between relationship time, with the exception of one—casual sex. Despite what I watched on *Sex and the City*, sleeping around held little appeal for me. Salsa shot through the paradigm of the lonely single woman. I had found a way station, a place between the struggle of dating in LA (a well-worn cliché) and a life of celibacy. I now had a place to take my sexuality without fear of pregnancy, disease, or the existential despair of a bad date. I could dance, feel a man's touch, feel pretty, and go home without any negative repercussions. For the first time, I began to separate the act of sex from the sexual energy that flowed through me, and I questioned how much of the actual physical experience of sex I had ever wanted in the first place. Salsa felt so good, it felt like enough. I felt fully satisfied to live in the energy of my femininity, the space between the spark of life-giving energy and actual physical intimacy.

Salsa World was, if nothing else, a world of boyfriends. Not real boyfriends, as in the guy who takes you to dinner and a movie or the guy with whom you do exclusive activities, like have sex or cuddle. You might do these things, but so long as a woman views a salsa guy's role in her life as that of a friend and a dance partner, he can do no wrong. He can't cheat on her because they aren't together, and she doesn't care what he's doing when he's not dancing with her. She knows he enjoys dancing with her, or he wouldn't keep coming back. And he will certainly try to show her a good time for all of the three to six minutes of the song. However, if she chooses to take the relationship outside of the salsa club and impose any kind of traditional boyfriend/girlfriend scenario, all bets are off.

A dance partnership is not unlike a real relationship; there's reciprocity, mutuality, and the gradual building of trust over time. There might be "salsa chemistry" or utter repulsion. The same things happen in salsa dance relationships that happen in regular relationships. Sometimes they end suddenly, in a big movie star tabloid breakup, or gradually, over time, like two people who drift apart. Some last for years, and some for weeks. Some are boring but stable, some exciting and unpredictable.

Like with all relationships, we walk into a partner dance with hope and blinders, seeking bliss, but as we develop as dancers, or life experience, it gets harder to find that match. The person who hears the music the same, leads or follows with symmetry, and smells tolerable.

Dance partners are not real boyfriends. Hanging out with a salsa guy is not the same thing as a date. At least, in theory.

I first danced with a young man I knew only as Short Hat Guy in the early days of my recovery from the flu from hell. The normal turmoil of illness was exacerbated by the despair I felt when I thought about all the salsa I missed.

Short Hat Guy insisted on nailing every beat of a fast song while I panted.

"Again?" he asked when the song was over.

I couldn't make it through the second song without gasping for air. "I have to go home," I told him while I collapsed into a chair. It was only eleven o'clock at night, barely the salsa-witching hour, but I had no strength and had to go to work the next day.

"Can I get your phone number?" he asked.

"Maybe. What's your name?"

"Guillermo."

"How old are you?" I asked.

"Twenty-seven," he answered.

He looked about twenty-three at most. We might have been the same height.

"You think I'm some wetback, don't you," he said.

"No…not at all…no."

A "wetback" is a racist term for a recent immigrant from Mexico. No, I did not apply that word to him, but I did think he was far from "appropriate" for my dating demographic, an assumption that contained a dissertation worth of prejudice and judgment. And he called me out on it.

"I am too old for you."

"How old are you?"

"Thirty-four."

"You look young."

I gave him my phone number out of guilt for my prejudice and because I love hearing that I look young. I gave my number to lots of guys in my early days of salsa before I realized that I (a) didn't have to and (b) received so many uninspired text messages, such as "hi." Lisa once got a message from a salsa guy that said, "I'm bored."

"Do you think I have any game?" he asked with an air of serious concern.

"Sure, you have game," I lied. This guy has no game whatsoever, I thought.

Guillermo became my first steady dance partner. He danced with me every Sunday, taught me dance moves, and tried, in vain, to keep me on the beat.

Every beginner salsera needs her first Salsa Boyfriend, the guy with whom she feels comfortable enough to dance with all night. But like any nebulous relationship, the connection can become rife with confusion. For a woman who loves to dance, meeting a man within the confines of salsa music can overwhelm the senses. A moment of connection is created, however illusory, and a wonderful feeling emerges, born from an ambience created by intoxicating music. Sometimes I watched girls dance with their eyelids half closed, smiling. They looked like they just took ecstasy.

In retrospect, my first dance partner was a mere novice. But that's why I liked him. Guillermo had no game.

Game belonged to Ruben and the Ninjas, who fell in the category of Hot Player Salseros. Those dancers blessed with good looks and a fun personality. Not to be confused with the Predatory Salseros, who could be found all over salsa (and the world). A classic predator was not necessarily the greatest, most high-profile salsero, although he could be professional or, as in one notorious case, a famous teacher, like Alex Da Silva.[1] I later learned of multiple stories of teachers who harassed or assaulted students. As the consciousness of the #metoo movement progressed a decade later, those became far fewer. But salsa predators, like predators everywhere who look on from the outskirts and dark corners of clubs, were a reminder to me that salsa is the real world.

---

[1] Famous teacher Alex DaSilva was convicted for the rape of several female students and served time. Long before #metoo many women and men outed male dancers on Facebook for their behavior toward women.

SALSA CHICA

My friend Charles, a professor of comparative literature, once recounted a situation he witnessed with a teacher.

"A girl had just come by and said 'hello' and gave him a hug. After she left, he turned to me and another guy and said, 'I'm too nice to them, and they get attached…'"

I suppose Guillermo was still figuring out his approach. But I might classify him as a Relentless Salsero, the guy who likes the chase, if only because he danced with me for months. While I enjoyed dances with a fun young man, he worked his non-game.

One night, between dances, we talked for the first time, and he told me that he lived with his parents, brothers, and sisters.

"Don't you want your own place?" I asked. In my world, pre-California housing crisis, life led up to two states: single or cohabitation with a mate.

"I used to live with a friend, but then I got a DUI," he said matter-of-factly. "I needed to hire a lawyer, so I moved back home to save money."

"Any plans to go to school?"

"No, I don't really like school."

DUI. No education. Lives at home. It seemed that my dating pool had changed since I graduated from Yale. Up until I turned thirty, I dated guys with good jobs, nice cars, and a tendency to pick up the sushi check. (I got dessert.) However, while many of those boyfriends looked great on paper, some had issues that did not make it to their résumés. For a year and a half, I dated a music attorney, Michael, who loved me and wanted to marry me. He told me that he once managed to get a DUI cleared from his record with his respectable connections. That's the difference between a guy with a good job and one who lives with his immigrant parents. One can make the DUI disappear. The other has to work three jobs to pay for a lawyer and pray that the judge likes him.

Then again, perhaps my dating pool had not really changed.

One day while at work, my 2005 Nokia blasted its loud air raid sound to indicate that I had received a text.

"I think I have a text message!" I announced proudly to whoever might listen. I checked my phone to find a number not in my contacts.

"What do you want from me this Valentine's Day? A. Nothing B. Hug C. Kiss D. Roses E. Sex F. Money"

"R u talking to me?" I replied.

"Yes. Who else?"

Your entire female contact list?

"JK! But out of curiosity what would u pick?"

"Salsa dance and a hug," I responded while I looked up "JK" in the Urban Dictionary.

"Good answer."

Despite the sweet eighth grade exchange, I could not fathom spending Valentine's Day with Short Hat Guy. Sure, I was riddled with loneliness, but he was eleven years my junior.

A few hours later, while still at work, I found myself in a meeting with Bill, the fifty-three-year-old

SALSA CHICA

white programmer whom I referred to as Evil Flash Programmer in my blog. He and the director of technology had gathered around my desk to discuss a crisis of programming code. They may as well have been speaking Arabic for all I understood what they were saying.

"Then maybe you should learn Arabic," said Evil Flash Programmer when I mentioned this to him.

When they were done, Evil Flash Programmer approached my desk.

"I believe it was Kant or Buddha who said, 'Every day you wake up, and everything is fucked.'"

We spent the rest of the day huddled around his computer. "So, are you dating anyone?" he asked.

"The majority of guys I meet are salsa dancers whose idea of commitment is two songs in a row."

"Maybe you're being too picky," he said. "And a little judgmental. I didn't find someone until I stopped worrying about the type of person I should be with and focused more on how I felt around her."

Evil Flash Programmer had found his fiancée through an "international dating site" and was on his second Brazilian girlfriend. His first girlfriend's low voice sounded to him like she might have had a sex change operation. Now he was in the process of waiting for the papers to clear for Andressa while he sent her whatever he could spare from his paycheck. Not exactly a dating guru, but he did have a point.

"So," I finally responded, "what you're saying is that I shouldn't, hypothetically speaking, write off a twenty-four-year-old, five-foot-four, slightly overweight guy because he lives with his parents, isn't a legal resident, and believes that salsa is his ticket to infinite possibilities of unattached sex, which it probably is?"

"I didn't know you were into short, fat guys. Otherwise, if you like him, why the hell not?"

Evil Flash Programmer's words stayed with me the next time I saw Guillermo. For six months Guillermo danced with me every Sunday night, taught me new moves, kept me on the beat, and reprimanded me for spinning out of control. He may not have looked good on paper, but who wants to go to bed with a résumé?

However, he started to exhibit one trait that set me ablaze for any man: he started to ignore me. He had received my friend zone kibosh and incorporated it into his salsa ritual. And then, like a stereotypical woman, I really liked him.

One night after hours of sweat-drenched salsa at Mor Bar, he walked me to my car parked on Main Street in Santa Monica. He looked around the empty sanitized street like it was a different country.

"The people in my community are different than the people in there," he said waving to Mor Bar. "In my community the people are ignorant."

On Sundays I sometimes biked to the Farmer's Market a few blocks away where moms bought four dollar peaches and J.Crew families lolled about the grass with their strollers, organic arugula, and wheat-free pancakes. I never felt more Mexican than Sundays in Santa Monica.

"The people here are ignorant, too," I replied. "Just in a different way."

We stopped by Guillermo's Honda. The driver-side door was red, but the rest of the body panels belonged to the original forest-green car. Except for the roof, which was white. The car had clearly been Frankensteined together from various vehicles.

"It's the colors of the Mexican flag," he said.

"Very patriotic," I commended.

"I built the engine myself. In my neighborhood, everybody knows how to fix cars."

When my car broke down, I gave someone money until it started again. What happened in-between remained a mystery.

Shortly, thereafter, he came over to my place and stayed the night.

"I kind of want to see him again," I told my therapist. I noticed her new pedicure. She wore a beige sweater while I sat on her beige couch underneath a Georgia O'Keefe print.

She made a smiley "good for you" face.

"I feel like, I don't know, like I could be with him all the time."

"It sounds like falling in love."

Love? Ugh. No.

But I had to acknowledge that I liked him. Unlike the Ninjas, Guillermo danced with any and all women: the old ladies, the large roly-polies, and those of all cultures and skill level. He was an equal opportunity salsero.

The truth is that Guillermo was a good guy. He spoke a lot about his neighborhood and community and placed a great value on relationships.

"Sometimes I pay for things with a favor. Like, if a friend helps me move, I'll fix his car. I think it's better because it creates a relationship and makes you more connected to the people around you."

In the world I lived in, people paid each other to be left alone and then paid a therapist to examine the existential loneliness.

Not without ambition, he had graduated from two fire academies as part of his efforts to become a fireman. I imagine he did not make the cut due to his height.

My therapist told me to "give myself permission" to date (sleep with) a guy eleven years my junior.

"Chica, he's adorable," said Lisa. "He's a mensch."

Sometimes he emailed me poems and thoughts throughout the day. Hormones overtook my brain. What a judgmental bitch I had been to say no to someone so wildly inappropriate for me.

But then one night, when I saw him in salsa, he danced two songs and then disappeared. I watched him dance all night with another girl. One night she was a beautiful brunette; the next night she was white, blond girl. It did not matter, she wasn't me.

"But that's just salsa," said Lisa. Right, that's just salsa, I told myself over the summer. One night we sat in his tricolored car and talked about his estranged father.

SALSA CHICA

But when I saw him out, I was just a dance partner. Not even one of his top Myspace friends.

I struggled with this, like most women in and outside of salsa. Years before "ghosting" became a colloquial term, I was "salsa ghosted." And then one day he danced with a short white girl…all night. She was his age and even shorter.

He had a girlfriend.

"Oh, Chica, he's just a kid," said Lisa.

It was no surprise to me that my love affair with Guillermo ended before I realized it had even begun. I tried to be mad at him, but deep down I got it. Guillermo had been sent by The Salsa Welcoming Committee.

My affair with salsa had just begun.

Chapter 5
The Relentless Salsero

Step 5: Vow never to date a salsero again.

Dancing is a perpendicular expression of a horizontal desire.
—George Bernard Shaw

Salsa music, in the early years, affected me like champagne. It made life resplendent. The sounds of Johnny Polanco's saxophones and trumpets hit my bloodstream and changed the chemistry of my brain the second I entered Monsoon's cavernous room. Dimly lit and covered in twinkling lights, Monsoon felt otherworldly. Unhappiness, resentment, and office drudgery fell away as my body filled with the sounds of joy.

In this environment, I opened up to life and new people, many of whom happened to be men. I first met Raul, a fair-skinned, forty-year-old, Nicaragua-born man with green eyes and a meticulous *GQ* style at Monsoon. Kind and deferential, he danced multiple songs with me and then insisted on walking me to my car.

"He's relentless," I told Lisa. From then on, we referred to him as "Relentless."

Relentless was not a great dancer. He never will be. He lacked the requisite desire to cultivate footwork or practice his spins. With his lack of ego, he stood apart from the salseros who seemed driven to impress with their "shines." However, what he did in the way of dancing did not always fall into the category of "salsa." But back then, I didn't know enough about the parameters of LA Style Salsa dancing to understand that slithering down a woman's body and then back up again while making a sexy face is not a "salsa move."

A few weeks after we first met, Relentless sat down next to me on a bench at Mor Bar. I tried not to watch Guillermo dance with his new girlfriend.

"I feel a lot chemistry," he said, after a few minutes. "And would like to have sex with you," he added, as if he were discussing Thai food.

Compared to current dating app culture, Relentless's blatant sexual overtures seem quaint, even Victorian. To his credit, Relentless felt no need to create a pretense. He did not hold back his true intentions, thoughts, or feelings. He approached sex with honesty and forthrightness: he was a man looking to get laid.

"Listen, I'm not like all *these guys*," he said, waving toward the dancers on the floor. "They will tell you anything to try to sleep with you. Like, 'You're so beautiful.' 'You're so cute.' 'You're so fun to dance with.' That kind of thing."

"Yes, that would be terrible."

"I'm just being honest about who I am, because I don't want to be like all *these guys*."

In the coming months, I would hear more about *these guys*. It would soon become apparent that Relentless felt deeply disturbed by a population of salsa guys whose motives so resembled his own. These guys, like Relentless, were not here to build relationships but, unlike him, lacked the courage to admit it.

"Well, I'm not really looking for casual sex," I confessed. "I'm more of an emotionally avoidant relationship girl."

After my experience with Guillermo, I had tabled sex for a steady rotation of dances with guys whose lead I could tolerate. Salsa seemed like the perfect safe substitute to hook-up culture. All the slime and sweat, with none of the disease or pregnancy.

"It could turn into a relationship. But I'm not going to promise you anything," Relentless cajoled one night, as if this were the sticking point upon which the future of our relationship rested.

Similar conversations took place over the following months, weeks, and, yes, years.

"Seriously, why won't you sleep with me?" he asked me one night when I accepted his offer to walk me to my car. "Are you in love with someone? I've been around the salsa scene for ten years. I've seen it a million times. The guy pursues the woman for months…"

"Like what you're doing…"

"*Except* I'm honest. I'm not telling you all of these *lies.*"

"Like, I'm beautiful and all that horrible stuff."

"What I'm trying to say is that I've seen it a million times," he continued. "The girl starts to like him, fall in love with him, believe all the bullshit he tells her about how much fun it is to dance with her, until…*bam!*…he gets what he wants."

I wondered if I had just been a pawn in Guillermo's game of having no game. I had felt superior to him, even sorry for him. But in the end, I had just been another victim of the double-edged salsa sword.

"Who is he?" Relentless asked one night about the mystery man who kept him from my bed. "Were you dancing with him tonight? Was he that Mexican-looking guy?!" he said in disgust.

"What do you have against Mexicans?" I asked.

While Relentless's attitude disturbed me, it was not unusual in my experience to hear a fair-skinned Latino look down on darker pigmentation.

"You know, every salsera is in love with one salsero."

"Says who?"

"Oh, come on! You know how many girls I'm friends with?"

"You mean 'friends,'" I said while I gestured dramatic air quotes. "I'm sure they are all very meaningful friendships…"

In all fairness, Relentless did have many female friends. He liked women. He also liked gossip. In many

SALSA CHICA

ways, he reminded me of an under-stimulated housewife who needed a little scandal in the neighborhood to stay interested in life.

"And what about every salsero?" I asked. I was again avoiding the question. "Are they in love, too?"

"They're in lust…with however many…depends on the guy, the time, the age…you know. You think these guys are here for *dancing*?"

"Uh, well…yes," I said. I didn't go into Angel's theories. Relentless fell into a different category of men who never cared about dancing, who loved the music but mostly the women.

Eventually, I came to learn how things worked, ideally, in Relentless's world. He—the relentless salsero—goes out into Salsa World on a regular basis and meets many women. Eventually, one or more become his "friend." A "friend" to Relentless is a woman he finds attractive and engaging. Would Jesus call this friendship? Probably not. But he probably also wouldn't call it "dating" either.

There's such a paucity of appropriate language for the endless variety of relationships present in post-marriage society: Companion, Wife, Girlfriend, and Friend simply don't cut it anymore. What about Guy I Dated for Six Months and Now We're Friends, which is an entirely different relationship from Friend I Would Like to Date, or, in my case with Relentless, Lonely Guy Who Can't Relate to Women Other Than as Sexual Objects Who I Hang Out with Because I'm Lonely Too. In other words, a "friend." So, I'm stuck with this very

Hello Kitty word for something fundamentally lacking in innocence.

Regardless, in the course of this "friendship," Relentless approached the prospect of both parties sleeping together much like you might discuss going to see a matinee. Just something to, you know, relax and get to know each other better. If one party gets too attached, well, you can't say she wasn't forewarned. If both parties get attached, hey, there's no problem. And, if Relentless gets attached, well, he can handle it. Maybe.

"Sometimes I'll think I don't feel anything for a girl, and I'll see her dancing with somebody, and I'll feel so jealous that I'll want to kill the guy."

Such rare occurrences aside, once the sexual act had lost its fun and exciting properties, Relentless somehow managed to coax said woman out of his life to the degree to which he could eventually venture back out into Salsa World, free and unattached.

However, this plan sometimes backfired.

"Sorry, I didn't make it tonight," he said over the phone one morning after he failed to show up at Monsoon the night before. "Francisco told me that my stalker was there." Francisco was a promoter and, apparently, a repository of information on Relentless's many salsa indiscretions.

"Which one?" I asked him later. As I learned, there were more than a few old embers fuming around Salsa World in search of Relentless. In fact, Salsa World could be described as one large smoldering piece of lava.

SALSA CHICA

"I wouldn't judge you if you decided to sleep with him," Lisa said one night as we ate appetizers at the Monsoon happy hour before the salsa music began. "Because he's good looking and why not?"

Relentless did look good. He dressed well and said funny things, and I felt some fondness for him. But other than that, all he seemed interested in talking about was sex and the behavior of "these guys."

"When guys ask me if I've slept with you, I say 'No,'" he shared in a tone that suggested that this admission rivaled the moral integrity of Gandhi.

"That's because you haven't slept with me."

"And that's what I say. I say, 'No, I haven't slept with her.' Even if I have slept with a girl, when a guy asks, I still say, 'No.'"

One Friday evening he called and asked if I wanted to come over for a piece of Bundt cake. I had nothing else to do and felt intrigued by Relentless's hobby. He baked?

The first thing I noticed was how his apartment seemed to have leaped directly out of the Pottery Barn catalogue.

"I like the wall fixtures," I said as I ate Bundt cake and watched him iron his pants. Ironing? He was getting ready to go to Steven's Steakhouse with Francisco. He didn't like Steven's because, in his words, it was "so ghetto," but he had nothing better to do.

After that night, I started to wonder about his sexuality. He constantly talked about his long history of conquests, the notches in his belt, and his list of "stalkers" (aka, former victims). But it wasn't the first time I suspected a salsa guy of overcompensating for some unconscious "man love" through aggressive sexual advances toward women and multiple sexual partners. I noticed presumed heterosexual salseros watch each other dance, they seemed captivated by each other's bodies. Salsa allowed the expression of many latent feelings.

I wondered if Relentless pursued me to avoid his homoerotic feelings.

But I had to admit my own part. I basked in his desire, feeling the power of the pursued. I committed the cardinal sin of women—the "cocktease." I wondered, however, if he just enjoyed the status quo; after all, a relentless salsero, by definition, gets off on the perpetual chase.

I had to admit that a part of me craved the constant never-ending validation of Relentless's sexual interest.

But vanity has its limits. We had reached the end of our relationship rope, and I began to experience Relentless fatigue. I could no longer be his object of lust. But instead of telling him, I practiced my nonverbal avoidant techniques, perfected in and out of salsa. The old "refusal to make eye contact" or "hello with no hug" usually sufficed to ward off unwanted dance requests and other offers.

However, Relentless was not one to be deterred by such obvious passive-aggressive behavior. Life as a relentless salsero had helped him build immunity to such tactics long ago.

SALSA CHICA

"Listen, stop avoiding me. I know you're not going to sleep with me. OK? I want to be your friend. Now will you dance with me?"

After that, he seemed to have accepted the nonnegotiable parameters of our relationship. In fact, he seemed to have relented. A few nights later, I ran into Relentless/Relented, and he offered to walk me to my car.

"How do you women do it? How do you go so long without sex?" he asked me once we arrived to my car.

"If I'm not in love with the person, it's just not fun… certainly not worth it."

The reality of pregnancy and disease seemed far from his mind. But, nonetheless, Relented thought for a moment.

"Maybe I do want a girlfriend. In salsa everyone is with everyone else, one way or another. I want to feel something for someone besides just lust."

For a moment, I questioned my acceptance that Relented was a hormonally driven teenager with a calcified heart in the body of a forty-year-old man. In some ways, I regarded salseros like nonhuman beings, as I had with so many boyfriends.

"I want to tell you something," he said, looking at me very seriously. "I loved my grandmother. But one time she said something that made me really angry and sad. She said that the only man she had ever been with was my grandfather."

"What's wrong with that?" I asked. "Some might find that romantic."

"The guy was an asshole. He was like all 'these guys,'" he said waving toward the now desolate club.

"It broke my heart. Because I wish she could have experienced something good. So, what I'm telling you is that you need to find a guy who is not a salsa dancer. Someone outside of this scene. Someone who is nice to you, with whom you can have sex. That would be good for you. That is what I want for you."

He gave me a big hug, kissed my cheek, opened my car door, and made sure that I had my seat belt on. It took me years of experiences later to realize that Relentless really was a friend.

Chapter 6
What a Feeling!

Step 6: Live the dance movie.

Those who dance are considered insane by those who cannot hear the music.

—George Carlin

First salsa dance team led by Christian Oviedo, 2007

I never understood my desire to dance salsa. But I just went with it. For my entire adult life, up until I found salsa, I had allowed my linear mind to dictate my choices. My brain went to Yale, wrote resumes and blogs, found jobs, paid bills, told me who to date, and to buy eggs at Trader Joe's but fruit at Whole Foods. I could rely on reason to make good decisions about life's practicalities. But my body yearned for something else.

When I started to dance, I threw out all conventional ideas of happiness in America—success, wealth, family—but the bare necessities of adulthood: a job to pay the bills. I only wanted to dance. While my friends used their bodies to make new humans, I used mine to body roll. We were all transcending our bodies in a way. However, my married friends went down the traditional American story, the pursuit of domestic bliss. Meanwhile, I lived the Dance Movie.

I don't know the exact origins of the Dance Movie, but I assume it began in the '70s, around the time of *Saturday Night Fever*, the classic film about a working-class Italian who crosses a literal bridge of class boundaries through the dance of disco. Before the Dance Movie, musicals occupied the cultural space that celebrates dancing. I love musicals. I wish my life were a musical. But the classic, weird tenet of musicals is that everyone already knows how to dance and sing.

In the Dance Movie, the act of dancing is something to be learned, perfected, or honored. It is a sacred activity that eclipses everything else in the lives of the main characters. Even if they suck. Skill level does not matter because the vital arc of the Dance Movie rests on the transformation of the characters through the act of dancing.

In *Dirty Dancing*, Baby, played by Jennifer Grey, grows out of the value system of her upper-middle-class family after her working-class boyfriend, Johnny Castle, played by Patrick Swayze, says the famous, awful yet awesome line, "Nobody puts Baby in the corner." She then publicly leaps into his arms, thus creating a new ritual at wedding receptions. At the end of the movie, Baby is no longer a compliant daughter but a woman who understands the dark truths of life, the class divide around her, and her place in it. Her love affair with Johnny does more than just lift her up in the air, it helps her break free. Through her dance journey she becomes her own person. In *Footloose*, Kevin Bacon's character asserts his spiritual right to dance in an oppressive Christian community that vilifies it. And in *Flashdance*, Jennifer Beale's character lives a double life as a welder and stripper/burlesque dancer (still not sure what to call it). Usually, characters change culture or classes, and the whole thing culminates in some big finale. Whatever the story, certain themes remain consistent across a wide variety of Dance Movies, including one, if not all, of the following:

1. THE REVOLUTION: The struggle between society and the heart. Through the act of defending the right to dance, or to embrace a personal

style, the protagonist resists the norms and precepts of their society. This character arc can be seen in *Strictly Ballroom* and *Footloose*.
2. THE LOVE STORY: An interracial or cross-class love story that forces the community to confront its prejudice or racism. This storyline can be seen in movies like *Dirty Dancing*, *Breakin'*, and *Save the Last Dance*.
3. THE CHEESY SCRIPT: With a few exceptions, Dance Movies, like salsa, are often woefully lacking in irony. But seriously, nobody should put Baby in the corner.

My Dance Movie journey began after I threw down the $115 for the shoes. I knew there was no going back. I don't remember if I told my mother about the salsa shoes or how much I paid for them. But I did feel scandalous, like I was breaking every rule of life. How would salsa make me successful? What would I gain? All I knew was that I wanted to dance, and if I didn't do it at 34, then when would I do it?

I never danced to get in shape or look better, but according to the people around me I looked far younger. I think by younger, what they meant was "thinner" and "happy." I felt so different about my life. Like I had something to live for. And I wasn't alone.

In those first few years, I met a lot of women and men who, like myself, structured their lives around salsa club nights, socials or classes. For Lisa and me, our lives

SALSA CHICA

revolved around Casa Escobar and Monsoon. On most Saturday nights we arrived at Monsoon just after 10:00 pm and stayed until the DJ played the last song, usually Hector Lavoe's classic ballad, "Todo Tiene Su Final" (Everything Comes to an End). The song served as the DJ's signal that the night was over and we should all go home. But Lisa, a handful of hard-core salsa stragglers, and I ignored the song's message. After the song ended, we begged for one more. And one more after that. On more than one occasion, Guanajuato chanted "*Otra! Otra!*" (Another one! Another one!) At which point the DJ played one or two more songs. After which Lisa, Amy, and I stood around longer, like girls who didn't want to go to bed. That is, until we saw that the staff needed to go home.

"There's nothing dignified about this," Lisa said one night.

Every Saturday night was prom.

Afterward, we took off our shoes and put on our UGG boots or sandals. We allowed escorts to walk us to our cars in the barren, lonely parking lot. Sometimes Lisa or Relentless drove me to my car, and we sat in our cars and talked about salsa. I went home and slept like a rock. I danced myself into exhaustion and out of depression or illness. With my body filled with endorphins, I rarely got sick. Even with the exchange of bacteria with a few dozen partners. For all I know, salsa gave me more antibodies.

"This is the happiest time in my life," Lisa said one night as we left Monsoon. "I always loved dancing. And I loved men. But in salsa, I have dancing and men."

Like most people in LA, Lisa had no appreciation for the benefits of aging. However, the power of salsa mollified her distress to an impressive degree.

"I only pray every day that I can just stay healthy enough to dance salsa for a few more years."

During the first few years, nothing thrilled Lisa more than a dance with one of the Ninjas. When she did, she made sure to tell everyone.

"I just danced with Ruben!" she said after rushing up to me. "I almost died." Then she threw in her classic descriptor, "He's *gorgeous*!"

Lisa found many men in and outside of salsa "gorgeous." She never went home with anyone but pawed the Ninjas or Ruben like puppies.

"They're like toys to me," she said. "You should have seen me in my forties!"

"You won't be able to do that when you're married," I warned.

"I can't help it," she replied. "I'm just visual."

However, there was one salsero who stood above the others in Lisa's eyes. Actually, he literally stood a good six inches above a community of medium- to small-sized men and women. For mysterious reasons, salsa attracts smaller people, and anyone over six feet towers over the dance floor. Pablo, a tall, lanky Latino, looked like Elvis and possessed the faultless characteristic of saying the right thing to any and all women.

"You look beautiful to me as always," he said to me one night.

"Thank you," I replied.
"What did he say to you?" asked Lisa.
"He said 'You look beautiful as always.'"
"That's what he said to me!"

Pablo failed to discriminate, but nobody minded. His words proved the Dance Movie tenet of a terrible script.

"I want to come back in my next life as Pablo's wife," Lisa said one night.

"Lisa, Pablo will never have a wife," I said. "Not in this life or any other."

"Damn…you're right."

Early on I often felt like Blanche DuBois, but Lisa's teenage-girl enthusiasm inspired me to follow my passions well into my fifties or longer.

Although Lisa had worked as a professional jazz dancer, she did not pick up salsa right away. In fact, you could say that she and salsa had a struggle. Some salsa guys patiently led her. But she persevered. Lisa made enough money to hire teachers for private lessons. She practiced at home. She practiced the basic alone at clubs. We hosted workshops in her apartment and mine. Anytime I learned a new move, I went into the back room at Monsoon and taught it to Lisa. Nothing solidifies a lesson like teaching it, and Lisa and I lived for new moves. Still, she seemed to suffer from a severe case of white girl's disease.

One night she ran up to me after a song ended.

"I just felt salsa *in my body*…I'm not even drunk!"

I knew what she meant. Salsa changed my body chemistry. But unlike red wine, salsa left me with more energy and clarity. It seemed almost like a food group I had been starved for, and now I needed a large dose.

Unlike me who grew up among the Latino community, Lisa grew up in an upper-middle-class Jewish household in New York. Salsa introduced Lisa to a different culture, one that oddly fit her more than her own. When I watched her dance with Ruben or Milo, I saw a woman who had found her people.

We had both long since become clichéd salsa addicts. Our salsa schedules had gone from once a week at Casa Escobar to three to four nights a week.

"I lie in bed at night and think 'What is going to happen to me?'" Lisa confided to me one night. "This has taken over. It's like I joined a cult. What if I never get out?"

I, too, wondered how long I could keep this up. I often drove the two miles to my job and wished my commute were longer. I needed more time to apply concealer and maybe pass a comb through my hair. My lack of daytime personal care did not go unnoticed.

"It's called grooming," said Evil Flash Programmer one day.

"I'm not trying to impress anyone here," I explained. And, indeed, in addition to my nighttime dress standards, I lost interest in my daytime appearance. As my responsibilities grew as a project manager, I became even less feminine in appearance. I often led meetings, crammed into a tiny conference room with long-legged white guys. The testosterone overwhelmed me. I wore button-down shirts and slacks at work. I watched salsa videos and thought about dance moves all day as I glazed over schedules and budgets.

I lost interest in the guys at work, in their wire-framed glasses and band T-shirts, and anyone who could not lead me on the dance floor, a serious impediment to my chances of finding real love. I lived on the edge of exhaustion with a Sunday, Monday, and Wednesday night salsa schedule and a job where a departure before eight o'clock at night was seen as an indulgence on par with a personal day. I bought groceries on Saturdays and cleaned my apartment on Sundays. I could have rested on Saturday nights, but Lisa would not hear of it.

"Are we going to see you tonight?" asked Lisa on a Saturday afternoon.

"I don't know," I would say. "I'm very tired…"

"I'm going to take a salsa nap. And then, I want to see you there at ten."

If I didn't make it, she called me the next day.

"All the saul-seros were there…"

But I soon found that I did not have to just go out at night. One summer Saturday afternoon, I sat around in my apartment with nothing to do when a friend shared a Facebook post about a salsa event at the Los Angeles County Museum of Art. I spent the afternoon dancing outside to a live band. That summer I found live salsa music all over Los Angeles. On the Santa Monica Pier,

Burton Chace Park in Marina Del Rey, the Music Center in Downtown Los Angeles. We found that our favorite salsa bands performed at dozens of parks and outdoor venues. Friends invited me to the Oxnard Salsa Festival, where I baked under the hot sun to live music. Every event felt like a celebration of something. But what? For me, I celebrated that I could dance.

For many years in the 2000s, a dancer sacrificed his Venice house for a Fourth of July salsa party that, to the horror of his affluent neighbors, included three to four bands and several DJs. The party began around noon and continued until well after midnight or whenever the police showed up. The time became earlier and earlier as the neighbors lost tolerance for hordes of cars of mostly nonwhite salseros accustomed to dancing till five o'clock in the morning.

Years later I met a guy who just started to dance salsa. In his early forties, a white male therapist with gym rat arms.

"Last summer was my first summer of salsa. It was the best summer of my life."

In the first years of dancing I rarely drank alcohol. One glass of Chardonnay caused me to spin out of control. About three or four years into salsa, I attended parties hosted by my salsa friends that easily went till four o'clock in the morning. I found that the smallest amount of alcohol sped up the transport into what you might call "the zone." Dancers know this space well. I could arrive to this space without alcohol, but it might take longer. But a day of loneliness or sadness, or fatigue and discouragement, could transform in a moment into a complete immersion into the Salsa Zone.

I now believe that the ability to stay up to dance salsa till two o'clock in the morning had less to do with youth, energy, or health but the spiritual energy that comes from a desire to live. I knew people decades older than me who had stamina that made no sense when correlated to their age. Lisa started salsa at the age forty-nine and spent years staying out till two o'clock on weeknights. In time, when the love affair wore down, many of my friends marveled at the stamina that kept us going into the night despite early work schedules. It would not last forever, I discovered. It might come and go. But in the first blush of salsa love, I danced marathons, hit walls of fatigue, and then busted through them.

Whenever I got tired or worn down from the grind of work, the news, dishes, laundry, or bills, I knew that renewal in salsa would restore me. More important, I viewed my life as a sacred fact, to be lived and enjoyed as I desired. I felt agency and hope. Salsa broke me out of the matrix and gave me my own life.

The movie *Dirty Dancing* ends with a classic large dance finale. We don't know what happens to Baby and Johnny. Do they stay together? Does Baby fund more abortions? Does she continue to dance? All we know is that Baby grew up. Dancing was the foothold she needed to break away from the oppression she felt in her family. She got out of the corner. And so did I.

Chapter 7
Childless Spinster

Step 7: Defend the Salsa Lifestyle to your mother.

It has dancing in it...
　　　　　—Mom, talking about a terrible
　　　　　movie she wants me to watch

Mom and I, 1983

In the years that I danced, I felt happy or at least more content than ever before in my adult life. There was only one problem with my current brand of happiness: how to explain it to my mother.

"Who's that?" asked my mom.

"Oh, that's Faraz. He's a liver transplant surgeon for children. He plays salsa music in the operating room."

We sat in front of my computer at the kitchen table, where I gave her a photographic tour of my salsa life.

"Is he single?"

"Yes."

My mom pursed her lips, the way she did when I lost my retainers. Her daughter's misguided life, a trajectory of wasted opportunities.

"This is DJ Charlie…" I continued. "And that's Sung, he's researching a gene therapy treatment for HIV. They are both great guys."

"If they are so 'great,' why are they just your friends?!" she burst out.

"They're just dance partners," I offered meekly.

"I don't think you want a relationship!" she said in an accusatory huff and got up from the table.

If my salsa passion did not lead to a husband or grandchildren, she did not see the point. We had been here before. She held my relationship status on par with a chronic medical condition, something to research on the internet and discuss with her friends. She regularly lit candles for me at church.

SALSA CHICA

"My friends are lighting candles too," she told me one day.

"There are far more worthy causes of a candle vigil than my single status," I responded.

She kept lighting candles.

"You can light candles for me at church, but you can't set me up with any more sons of people you meet on cruises," I told her one day, after she got back from a cruise.

"You're not open-minded!"

"Stop yelling."

"I'm not yelling!"

"You have a yelling tone."

"Well, a 'yelling tone' is not yelling…"

I think most would agree that a "yelling tone" shares characteristics with "yelling," but my mother employed creative logic when it came to winning arguments. Most of our arguments ended with her saying, "Let me finish!" in a "yelling tone."

One such conversation revolved around vitamins. We had the exact same conversation for at least twenty years.

"How are you?"

"Tired."

"Are you taking vitamins?"

"No. I can't swallow them. They make me want to puke."

"Well, you can break them in half."

Over the years, the words remained the same, but the pitch increased.

SOLANGE CASTRO

"How are you?"

"Tired!"

"Are you taking vitamins?"

"No. I told you already. *Vitamins make me want to throw up!*"

"*Well, you can break them in half!*"

At this point, we had both reached a maximum "yelling tone."

But I did feel a premonition, a sense that these conversations, or arguments, were like the final wrapped Christmas gifts she gave me. A Crock-Pot or something else I never asked for and could not return. I knew she would not be here forever and I imagined that someday in the future I might wander down the Whole Foods vitamin aisle, feel a rush of wind through my hair, and hear a whisper say, "You can break them in half!"

Born in Bakersfield to migrant farmworker parents, my mother had spent her formative childhood in Rodeo, a small industrial town in the San Francisco Bay Area. After she graduated from high school, inspired by President Kennedy's famous words—"ask not what your country can do for you, ask what you can do for your country"—she volunteered to join the Peace Corp and spent two years in Northern Brazil. When she returned, she met my father at Merritt Community College, and they both attended the University of California, Berkeley, in 1968. During that time, she volunteered for Cesar Chavez, the famous Mexican American activist who unionized migrant farmworkers,

SALSA CHICA

and worked as an organizer in the boycott of grape growers in California.

After she and my father divorced, when I was five, she bought a house and worked at a nonprofit, where she helped new immigrants find jobs. Later she received her master's degree and wrote a book about Chicano folklore, a memoir of her childhood, and a novel. She inspired me to write and stood behind my creative efforts with the conviction of a general.

I grew up with a fun, adventurous mom. We planned movie nights and trips. I never saw the absence of a man in her life, minus my father who I saw regularly, as any impediment to her happiness.

One day she took me to the iron-on T-shirt store at a place we frequented called the "mall." I looked over a tall wall of designs before I found one of a fish on a bicycle.

"A Woman Needs A Man Like A Fish Needs A Bicycle…" I read. "What does this mean?"

"Well, does a fish need a bicycle?" she asked.

"No."

I was only ten, but the famous Gloria Steinem quote spoke to me. I loved it and had it ironed on to a jersey T-shirt. None of my fifth-grade friends understood it. Why would they? Why did I?

A few years later, at the age of fourteen, now covered in eyeliner and drenched in Jean Naté perfume, I came home one day to find my mom crying.

"I'm pregnant," she said.

She was forty-two. No IVF or hormone injections, just plain old irresponsibility. Eight months later I had a baby sister. My mother's boyfriend moved in, and our relationship was never the same. How could my independent mother trade in freedom and her feminist values for a marriage with an alpha male? In high school, I excelled in classes, sports and changing diapers. While my baby sister remains one of the greatest gifts from my mother, by the age of eighteen, I understood the realities of parenthood all too well.

Now in my thirties, I still believed a single life held possibility. I tried to quell my mother's concerns by telling her about my internet dates. One morning, after I returned to LA, I woke up to check my phone and found an email from her that began:

"At 4:00 a.m. this morning, I was thinking about online dating…"

Four o'clock in the morning! Talk about pressure. My singlehood not only drained her candle lighting budget but also impacted her sleep.

"Have you seen the movie Harold and Maud*? I just saw it again a few months ago—it's great. And Ruth Gordon is so wonderful. Check it out and view it again."*

My mother found my single life in my late thirties comparable to that of an eighty-year-old woman. If elderly Ruth Gordon could find someone, then surely, I could too.

"People love to talk about themselves, especially men…if you encourage them to talk about themselves, they'll be happy

SALSA CHICA

with you. Then you can say, 'Wow, that sounds interesting!' 'How did you do that?' Etc...."

My civil rights activist mother could now write for *Cosmo*.

However, her insistence that I feign interest in a man's conversation in order to "land him" seemed only a step above her other constant suggestion: an arranged marriage.

"Arranged marriages work out," she told me one day.

"Yes, if you're from India and super young and want an arranged marriage."

"I just don't want you be alone anymore."

Of course, my mother's concern came out of love, care, and her desire to be a grandmother. And, of course, I wanted to find a partner. I wanted love too. But since salsa came into my life, my feelings about my single status changed. If I never met a man, I would still always have dancing.

I did not mind the idea of aging with my mother. Free from all the complications, and myths that plague romantic/sexual relationships, the idea of taking care of my mom, a person I loved, seemed at the very least, true and real. The term "childless spinster" had always sounded to me like a lot of free time. A spinster is a woman too old to marry. But why didn't she marry? Because a man didn't want her, or because she valued her life?

I figured that since many women outlive men, someday my stepfather would die and I, the "spinster," and my mother would share guacamole and *New Yorkers* while I continued to date unavailable salsa guys. Forever single, I would at the very least have my mother back.

Chapter 8
Jazzy Mambo

Step 8: Dance "On 2."

When the music changes, so does the dance.
—African Proverb

Dancing at the Mambo Outlet social in Culver City, 2013

SOLANGE CASTRO

For three years, salsa consumed all my free time. If a dancer admitted to me that he or she went out five nights a week, I understood. I once met a dancer who danced salsa thirty nights in a row. My dance partner, Faraz, the liver transplant surgeon, once confessed to me at Monsoon that he had a scheduled surgery at six o'clock in the morning. I looked at my watch and saw that it was close to midnight. (This changed my view of surgeons.)

Salsa had the power to transform my emotional state and awaken me to joy. No matter how angry, depressed, discouraged, rejected, or encumbered I might feel, a few dances pushed the negativity away. However, like all drugs, in time, the Salsa Fix lost its potency.

By my fourth year of salsa, I had memorized the repertoire of most of my dance partners, many of whom had studied with the same teachers and executed the same five choreographed moves. Sometimes, while in the middle of a dance, I thought about my Trader Joe's shopping list or looked around to see who might have walked in. Songs and moves were burned into my muscle memory. I still loved to dance, but I needed a new challenge.

Around this time, a DJ known to play "jazzy" salsa, invited me to take his "On 2" class. On 2, also referred to as "mambo," is a style of salsa wherein dancers "break" or step on the second beat. Most of Los Angeles dancers broke on the first beat and were appropriately called, "On 1" salsa dancers. The one tiny difference of this dance style, the breaking on the second beat, separated this group and created another community, which may as well have danced a different dance, so little did they have in common with the Ninjas or fedora-clad salseros of Steven's Steakhouse.

On 2 dancers, the hipsters of salsa, eschew commercial "salsa romantica" for mambo on vinyl and looked down on the attention-grabbing flips and neck drops of the dancers at Monsoon.

"On 1 dancers are more commercial," explained Angel to me one night during a rare conciliatory moment. "They are like Abercrombie and Fitch. For On 1 dancers, it's all about their clothes, hair, and personal style. On 2 dancers don't need to express themselves with clothes. They're like, 'I dance On 2. That's how I express myself.'"

Only when I took DJ Jazzy Mambo's class at an English pub in Santa Monica did I understand Angel's description of On 2 dancing and my experience of music and salsa was forever changed. I entered into a new phase, or as Angel would say, "level," of salsa.

I have not written much about the music of salsa or mambo because, outside of three years of French horn lessons and up until I began to dance On 2, I understood very little about musicality or rhythm.

"Mambo" and "salsa" mean different things to different people and also have different definitions whether you are talking about dance or music. Mambo-style dance, not to be confused with The Mambo—the ballroom dance that Patrick Swayze and Jennifer Grey danced in *Dirty Dancing*—must be danced on the second beat. Salsa, however, can be danced on any beat. In terms of music, mambo, which sometimes sounds more like jazz, helped shape what we call "salsa" today. I look forward to a day when American academics study mambo and salsa the way they might classical music.

After DJ Jazzy Mambo's class, a small group of On 2 dancers arrived to drink Blue Moon on tap and dance amid a pool table and local bar flies.

For a long time, the On 2 dance crowd ignored me. No matter how many times I might introduce myself. Despite all this, I wanted to learn to dance On 2, and I wasn't going to let a bunch of snobs keep me from doing just that. My friend Sung, first introduced me to On 2, and for at least a year, he remained my only dance partner.

I gradually built the courage to drive to Steven's Steakhouse. Steven's sits off the Interstate 5 in the City of Commerce. The drive to Steven's Steakhouse required twenty minutes on Interstate 10 and then fifteen more on Interstate 5 for a Westsider, like myself. Stranded in the middle of nowhere (no offense City of Commerce), Steven's doesn't look like a hot place for anything, let alone salsa dancing. In an age of vintage chic, circa early 2000s, it was hard to believe that the kitschy '70s-style architecture, wall-fixtures, or French maid costumes the waitresses wore were not ironic, but the fact that they, most likely, were not only added to the mystique.

SALSA CHICA

The first time Lisa and I drove out to the City of Commerce she fell victim to one of her existential panic attacks at the Eastern/Atlantic exit intersection. While we sat at the light, she turned to me and cried, "This is my life?!" However, three years later she stopped saying things like, "My mother would turn in her grave if she saw me now." And as far as I could tell, that passed for happiness in Lisa's life.

On Sunday nights, Steven's opened up two rooms for dancing. While most "serious" dancers preferred to bask in the surreal glow of the large "ballroom," more casual dancers occupied the smaller dance floor to the right of the entrance within a circular Jetsons-style bar. On Sunday nights, the Jetsons room attracted a more partying, less-serious salsa crowd. But on Tuesday nights, it filled with Los Angeles's best dancers, most of who danced On 2.

Serious dancers spoke of Steven's as the Holy Grail of salsa music and dancing. The first time I entered the dark crowded dance floor, I felt a palpable energy as I watched dancers groove to the tunes of DJ Martin. His mambo music felt visceral, like I had fallen into a blue aquarium, enveloped by a substance that reconfigured the molecules of my body and the neural pathways of my brain. On a good night, I left in the same state with which I exit a Korean spa.

I sometimes went to Cock 'n Bull at eight o'clock for the class and then drove to Steven's and danced with any On 2 dancer who would have me. This is where The

Fire (because of course I had The Fire, why else would I be driving to City of Commerce at ten o'clock on a Tuesday night?) carried me past the awkward transformation of becoming an On 2 dancer.

It took six months for me to hear the music on this new beat and then another year before I understood the preference. My immersion into the On 2 world not only changed the way I danced but also how I heard the music. Like Angel, I now believed that On 2 dancers danced "badass." More importantly, I *felt* badass. No more Salsa Romantica, the maudlin ballads sung by macho men, for me. I now understood the importance of musicality.

However, dancing On 2 cut my potential dance partners down by 80 percent. I became increasingly pickier about the song and lead. I declined dance offers without compassion or remorse. I looked down on On 1 dancers. They weren't Servants to the Music. I became a "Salsa Snob." One night it occurred to me that my attitude had evolved into that of the "Beverly Hills Bitch" Angel had challenged me to become.

But there was no going back. And, yet, I felt the loss of my old salsa life. I missed the days when I went to Monsoon and danced with Guanajuato who "whooped and hollered" (Lisa's description) all night. But I no longer enjoyed the demanding lead of On 1, it now felt rough. Hitting the one beat hard also seemed ridiculous and passé. Like melodrama or mall bangs. I sometimes regretted going down the On 2 road. If I just contented myself with dancing On 1, like Lisa, I would have never

SALSA CHICA

lost my innocence and become a Salsa Snob. But such is grace of life that we can evolve and dance to a different beat.

Many dancers like Angel may have enjoyed dancing On 2 but resorted to On 1 as an acceptance of the predominant language spoken in the Los Angeles salsa scene.

"If you live in LA, you should dance On 1," asserted Angel. "If you live in New York, you dance On 2. I want to make a shirt that says, 'This is LA…Dance On 1, Bitch!" He wrote an exclamation point in the air. "Exclamation point."

I understood Angel's point. It's rude to treat the locals like degenerates. In Los Angeles, the language of salsa is On 1, and the On 2 dancers are like the colonizers who refuse to shop at the local marketplace.

My On 2 education marked a change not just in my dance but also my life. Unlike the flashy On 1 moves of traditional LA Style Salsa, On 2 lends itself to a more internal experience of the music. On 2 dancers sometimes talk about the "feeling" of the music, which explains why these dancers seemed less friendly; in the world of salsa, they are the introverts. Up until that point, I danced with a greater consciousness of what I looked like as a dancer. This tendency plagues so many people someone wrote a quote about it. On the spectrum of self-consciousness, On 2 moved me down the scale closer to the place where I lived in my own experience.

One night, I watched Angel as he danced. He still incorporated his own style, a kind of hip-hop fusion, and years of practice gave his moves fluency. But as I watched him, I noticed him switch between On 1 and On 2. Years of dancing On 1 and On 2 had sort of rendered him in the middle.

Was Angel off beat?

Chapter 9
Leopard Print Grandma

Step 9: Understand your dancing roots.

I would believe only in a God who could dance.
—Friedrich Nietzsche

My mother and grandmother, 1963

SOLANGE CASTRO

"You remind me of my mother," my mom said one day. "After she got divorced, she went out dancing three times a week."

"You mean it's genetic?" I asked. I felt a wave of relief. Something could explain the insanity of my chosen life.

"I guess it skipped a generation," she added.

My mother and my aunts, her two sisters, might get up and move around to music at family functions, but none of them ever ventured into the night alone. But after my grandmother, Dolores, divorced my grandfather, she went out with friends in the Mission District of San Francisco to dance on a regular weekly basis.

Dolores and my grandfather, Martin, migrated to California from Texas in the late 1930s to work as farm workers. They danced to Norteño music, a type of Mexican country music, and even some mambo. I once had my mom list the types of music they listened and danced to, which included: Flaco Jiménez, Los Dandys, Los Tigres del Norte, and even Pérez Prado, a Cuban pianist who helped turn mambo into a worldwide phenomenon in the 1940s. I'm sure I danced to some of the same songs at Steven's Steakhouse or at On 2 socials that my grandparents listened to in the '40s and '50s.

It breaks my heart that I don't have my grandmother here to ask questions of, like, "What music did you dance to?"

I remember my grandfather as a strong masculine "macho" man, who wore cologne, a pencil-thin mustache, and sang with Mariachi bands after a few too many shots of tequila. He possessed a lot of good qualities, marital faithfulness notwithstanding. But he could dance. I imagine that if he lived in Los Angeles I might find him at Steven's with a three-piece suit and a fedora dancing in the corner.

It's the regularity of dancing that I shared with my grandmother—that, and our single status. She loved living alone. She once told me that it gave her a lot of "peace." After my grandfather, who can blame her?

Dolores never graduated from high school and had three kids by the age of twenty-one. By twenty-one I had my own dorm room. Despite the hard work of field labor, the responsibility of three daughters and a husband who came and went, my grandmother always looked like she had just stepped out of a fashion magazine or the *Mad Men* secretary pool. She loved clothes and regarded them as a way of self-expression. Whenever she helped me pack for a trip, we picked out an outfit for the plane (she would be horrified by sweatpants in economy). She wore a lot of leopard print, including three-inch heels (as her house slippers) well into her seventies. I have little patience for the female midlife crisis that begins at twenty-five. I had a sexy grandma.

For my fourteenth birthday, my grandmother bought me a paisley suit from Contempo Casuals, a haven of low-priced fashions in '80s malls. I probably wanted something from Esprit or Guess to wear with my espadrilles, as I aspired to look like a mean girl in an '80s movie. But when I opened the gift, my family of cousins and aunts "oohed" and "aahhed" and commanded me to change into it right then and there. Needless to say, in that moment, I hated them all.

Often any present opening met with a flurry of questions about the color.

"Would you call that? Vermillion?" asked my Aunt Elva.

"I think it's a Cinnamon," said Aunt Linda.

"No, I think it's a Cranberry," said Aunt Pat. While not really my aunt but my mother's best friend from high school, Aunt Pat showed up at all our family functions.

A discussion of colors worthy of the OPI nail polish writers' room followed, while I stood there in mortification and suppressed my urge to yell, "It's red!" Why do colors need names? I felt happy with Wet n Wild lipstick called #1952. After I changed into my new outfit, a discussion about my body ensued, to further deepen my mortification. I developed at a young age, a fact that made it acceptable to discuss my body as an entity separate from myself. There was love in these discussions, and internalized misogyny.

Despite a lack of what we might call "boundaries" today, I am so grateful that my mother and grandmother took hundreds of pictures because I see the love in their eyes for me and each other. They obviously adored each other. And I know they both had that love for me. I grew up being loved by very strong women and I can't help but believe that it shaped me into the person I am. Men come and go, but these women proved the true loves of my life.

My grandmother never asked herself, "Do I want kids?" or "Do I want to be married?" She had children before she stopped being one. Her role as a Mexican woman in her generation, economic class, and culture had defined limits and demands. Marriage was a necessity. After her kids were grown, she was done. She went dancing. Maybe I just picked up where she left off?

I might blame my grandma's dance genes and love for leopard print, but my dance roots extend to my paternal side. Steve, my dad, loves to dance. The fact that he loves to dance does not mean he knows what he is doing. Sometimes injuries are involved. Once, a whole tray of drinks went flying in the air. Another time he broke my mother's coffee table. He glued it together, and I use it today. If Steve wants to move his body, get out of the way.

When he was married to my mother, they danced together. He even went to Mexican clubs with my mother and my grandparents. As a kid, Steve danced with me at his many parties.

For years in my thirties, I did not speak to Steve. After he married a woman younger than myself, you could call our relationship "estranged" until one day, while home on a visit in Berkeley, I quite literally ran into him. While on a run I passed two cyclists. One of them made lingering eye contact.

"That looks like my father," I thought as I ran past them.

A few minutes later, the cyclist pulled up beside me.

"Hi, Solange!"

It was, indeed, my father. Steve.

"Hi!" I said. And I kept running. I didn't stop. I didn't even say "Hi, Dad." I just said "Hi!" I felt weird calling him "Dad" now that he had just married a woman younger than myself. It seemed maybe appropriate that I start calling him "Steve."

"How are you?" Steve asked, while biking alongside me.

"Good," I said.

Steve followed me on his bike for at least a mile. I kept running the whole time. However, I did accept his invitation to dinner and that begun the slow repair of our relationship.

I had spent most of my adult life feeling anger toward Steve. I blamed him for the fact that I could not attract a healthy partner. However, at a certain point, I realized that all the blame and anger clogged up my pipeline of energy, if not happiness. Salsa had helped unclog much of it, but now I had to do the rest. One night, many years ago, Steven listened to me cry about a recent break-up.

"Why don't you go out dancing?" asked my father.

"Dancing?!" I exclaimed as if he had just suggested I join the CIA—which he had on multiple occasions.

"Who am I going to go dancing with?"

He must have been in touch with something that only a parent can know because a few months later I drove myself to Casa Escobar.

And that is how it all began.

Chapter 10
Marriage vs. Salsa

Step 10: Partner with salsa.

To be fond of dancing was a certain step toward falling in love.

—Jane Austen

After I met Guillermo, I dated one other salsa guy. Our relationship followed the same salsa formula: man and woman dance, man and woman consummate, man dances with another woman, and woman fumes in the corner. After that I gave up on men in salsa as prospective partners. I satisfied myself with whatever happened on the dance floor.

But as I look back at my salsa years, one thing becomes clear: I did not have a lot of sex. As it turns out, *just* dancing with dozens of men was enough to satisfy that stadium-sized umbrella of needs that get lumped into the word "sex." Those include touch, attention, validation, and, at the end of the list, pleasure. In retrospect, salsa had so little to do with the bedroom. If I wanted sex, I would have found a boyfriend. I wanted salsa.

But even before salsa, I knew that a "casual" sexual lifestyle did not work for me. Despite the fun, frivolous nature of promiscuity as portrayed on shows like *Sex and the City*, the reality felt unsatisfying, at best. Unlike Samantha Jones, I was not written by a gay man. For one thing, casual sex requires more self-numbing than my snowflake sensitivity can tolerate. Then comes all the hormonal attachment that causes women like me adhere to men.

"It's the oxytocin," said Lisa to me one night when we lamented our addiction to a pastime that introduced us to an unavailable pool of men. She liked to follow the advice of a dating guru who advised women to think of themselves as "an egg."

But so long as we just wanted to dance, salsa did satisfy a lot of needs. Unlike the conjugal act, partner dancing requires next to nothing of either individual—a little trust and a sense of fun but certainly no dinners, talks about expectations, or therapy sessions. Certainly, no stressed-out drives to CVS for Plan B. Salsa proved not only the safest way to express my sexuality but also efficient and regret-free. Sometimes, it's enough to just look at the tiramisu.

After my second salsa romance turned into a real-life *Bachelorette* contest, I spent a lot of time talking to female friends, of all ages, whose salsa drama could easily fill two seasons of a Netflix show. It soon became

SALSA CHICA

clear, that most salseras would probably not find abiding love in salsa, unlike in the swing dance scene, where, according to a friend, more people found lasting love. Sure, some couples have emerged out of salsa, and I can count a dozen salsa babies. But while I could postulate a thousand theories as to why salsa gained the reputation as "not a place to date," I would say that the general ethos of joy and celebration, qualities associated to youth, make it attractive to those who want to avoid the harder parts of life: the tedium, grind, and Groundhog Day reality required to build a long-term relationship. Salsa is the fun of flirtation. Relationships, as anyone who has aspired to abiding love learns, challenge us to develop superhuman qualities of patience, forgiveness, and tolerance. Bor-ing!

I met a lot of women in salsa and became friends with some. I attracted a few college-aged female friends, who shared their stories of passion, betrayal, and the end-result of angry feelings that arise when treated like takeout food. I witnessed the jealousy and frustration that arose as naturally as heat when you meet men in a culture that permits them to change partners. Like much of the patriarchy, the formula for drama was built into the system.

"Wait, he didn't just dance with that girl three times in a row?!" said my friend Joanna one night. She was "seeing" Xavier, a twenty-six-year-old salsero and community college student. Joanna planned to get a master's in public policy.

"Is he dancing a Bachata with her?" Joanna lamented in my ear over the noise.

Bachata, a romantic style of music that originates in the Dominican Republic, had just begun to crop up in salsa clubs. Because Bachata is often described as a far "sexier" and close dance than salsa, some only dance it with their significant other.

"Hell no!" she continued. "…he didn't just get her phone number…"

Joanna called me one night to tell me that Xavier needed help in school.

"I can't believe I was up till one o'clock in the morning editing his paper," she said. "He can't write for shit. Listen to this, 'You people have a different life from me.' You people?"

Joanna made Xavier take an HIV test before she slept with him, which he obliged.

"The sex was terrible," she told me later. I've heard more than one salsera lament that chemistry on the dance floor fails to transfer to the bedroom.

I hardly felt like a role model. But she seemed to look to me for advice.

"One thing I've learned is never to have sex with someone unless you really want to," I said.

"Then I would have never had sex," she said.

I rarely met a woman not possessed by the perceived magnetic force of at least one salsero. Yet in time, it became clear that the magic came more from the music rather than the person.

SALSA CHICA

Despite my love and gratitude for salsa, I accepted that the realm of salsa, like most spaces in the world, belonged to men. Salsa was where they had the power to ask a woman to dance or initiate a relationship. That is, until I met Kim, a forty-five-year-old art director, who lived in Culver City.

"I've never been so slutty in my life," said Kim to me one night at the Warehouse, a small restaurant, also in Marina Del Rey, with a rented dance floor. I treated the Warehouse as a last resort for salsa on Friday nights, as the vibe of drunk salseros and overpriced drinks with umbrellas did not lend itself to my increasingly elitist dance sensibilities. If I was lucky, the smell of fried clams wouldn't make me hungry and/or nauseous, and a few good dancers might show up.

Kim and I had stepped outside onto the faux New Orleans ramshackle porch, which always reminded me of a line at Disneyland. We breathed the fresh air while I watched the koi fish in the pond.

"All these guys are really good for is dancing and sex anyway," she added.

I did not know Kim well but had struck up a conversation with her like I did with so many women in salsa. I craved understanding of what it was we were doing. A sort of "How is this ride working for you?" As a writer, the story of salsa fascinated me, and everyone had one. As a woman, their stories were also my own.

Kim who, like myself, was single and of an age where most of our friends were married, spoke openly with me.

I learned that Kim had entered into a series of "casual" relationships with at least three salsa guys.

"Don't you feel bad if you sleep with one of them, and then you don't hear from him?" I asked.

"Only if I don't have anyone else lined up," she replied.

She wasn't the first woman to turn the tables on the heterosexual paradigm of male privilege that permeated salsa. From what I saw and experienced, the sexual politics of salsa mirrored those of any patriarchal culture. I was conditioned to think of women as helpless victims, and men as sex-starved predators. With the help of Relentless, I had projected this paradigm onto Salsa World, where it seemed easy to imagine that the men, in control as they were as leaders, could prey on women looking for a good dance or a life partner.

However, even Relentless had mentioned meeting aggressive women who approached him for sex, which he happily obliged, but who sometimes made him feel "used." I wondered if Kim, at forty-five, was simply moving in that direction. Her behavior wasn't exactly that of a Cougar, the popular term for over-forty women who (in theory) preyed on younger men. She simply, as she relayed to me, did not refuse the sexual offers available to her.

"I figure this is the last hurrah before menopause," she added.

I began to wonder if Kim stood on the forefront of a movement. Maybe salsa was like the Ross of sex for single women. A place you went to when you needed a quick fix, something cute but cheap. You knew whatever you bought wouldn't last, but at least you didn't spend too much.

"But don't you wonder what they're doing out there when you're not around?"

"I'd rather just be in denial about it,"

"What if you actually start to like one of them?"

"I like all of them," she replied, again, as if we were discussing wine bars.

Like the character of Samantha Jones, who embraced her sexual and economic power by consuming men the way Carrie consumed her Manolo Blahniks, Kim had simply chosen the values and privileges of male sexual entitlement. Without a committed monogamous relationship, why not engage in casual sex in an environment that offers it as a post-cardio bonus?

Flash forward a decade later, and apps like Tinder make this chapter seem practically archaic. For women like Kim, sexual liaisons happened within the confines of a community with partners she might have known for months or years, people whose bodies and leads she felt comfortable and familiar with. Some of her partners even felt like close friends. Compared to the stone-cold booty calls with a stranger available through dating apps, salsa in retrospect looks like a safe place to pursue casual sex. And for Kim, this system worked.

The problem for me with casual sex came down to the same issue: what do you do when the party is over?

Discard said human being? How do you relate to someone you have slept with? You can't unsee or un-experience physical intimacy. According to those who practice polyamory, we can process and communicate our feelings into peaceful multi-union. But given the prevalence of "ghosting," most people can hardly manage one simple conversation. While it seems fair that women join the party men have enjoyed since time began, could this low bar of human conduct be considered "progress?"

On the other side of the paradigm lived my married friend Jessica in domestic bliss or boredom, depending on her mood that day. Jessica and her husband, Mark, grilled salmon before going to bed at nine o'clock at night like normal sane humans. Whenever I visited them, she set out a plate for me at the dinner table, like a niece or nephew.

"Dance for me," she said as I left her house to drive to a club in San Francisco.

And so I did. I danced for her and for all the mothers consumed with the work of raising another generation.

While I admired my mom friends, I never idealized the role. My mother did her part to dispel any fantasy I might have about marriage.

One weekend, my mom and her two sisters, my aunts, came and stayed with me in what a friend once referred as my "sanctuary by the beach."

"I wish I lived in an apartment by the beach by myself," said my eldest aunt, a veteran of a fifty plus year marriage.

SALSA CHICA

I love my apartment. The hardwood floors, high ceiling, proximity to the beach, and affordable rent gave me a place to write and just "be." Every relationship became a choice between a partner and my apartment. In seventeen years, the apartment is three and zero.

Of course, I had a natural distrust of marriage, which may have stemmed from a family that comes from several generations of divorce. But after a friend gave me the book *Marriage, a History*, by Stephanie Coontz, my skepticism only increased. From this book I learned many horrifying facts, like:

- Until the 1970s, a husband could force his wife to have sex whenever he wanted, by law.
- Under most legal codes, a husband didn't have to consult his wife about where they lived.
- The term "illegitimate" emerged so that the resulting prodigy of a one-night stand in a stony, Middle Age brothel couldn't claim rights to a family's estate.

Why had I not been taught this in school? What was calculus when compared to an institution that affects our day-to-day living for our entire lives?

And then I read a line toward the end of the book that I still have not recovered from:

When women marry, they typically do more housework than they did before marriage. When men marry, they do less. Marriage decreases free time for women, but not for men.[2]

In order to connect to another human being and feel the comfort of cohabitation, I would have to wash more dishes? Due to my Marie Kondo disease of order and cleanliness, I already felt that housework robbed me of so much time. If I got married, there would be only more human detritus to contend with. A cleaning lady could help with chores, but as I learned other scary terms like "emotional labor," the work of maintaining community and relationships, I started to rethink the paradigm of marriage in our current society.

I had done a good job of avoiding the issue of marriage through my twenties, but as I entered my mid-to-late thirties, the pressure increased.

"Just find an old, rich, bald guy," said my mother to me one day in all seriousness.

But it wasn't just my mother. I sensed an underlying subtext in the social circles that I didn't run in, so much as grazed, that the failure to make The Search for "The One" a priority, painted me as either weird, aloof, and/or self-indulgent. Most discussions about relationships inevitably resulted in some form of advice from a dating book. These nuggets included the following:

---

2 Stephanie Coontz, *Marriage, a History* (New York: Penguin Group, 2005), 312.

"You have to treat dating like it's a job."

"Dating is a numbers game."

"Make a list of what you want."

These suggestions, while wise and effective, also made dating seem as fun as a tax audit.

I felt lonely. But experience taught me that my loneliness came from something deeper than solitude. My personal emptiness had attracted equally impoverished men. Or worse, actors.

During one visit to Berkeley, two separate married-couple friends with whom I had scheduled dinner invited a surprise mystery guest, without any warning. Was my single company so loathsome to my couple friends that they must scramble through their single guy friends just to share some cider and fried calamari?

"You just don't seem like you're looking for a relationship," said a friend as we walked to the car.

I had to agree. I truly enjoyed my single life. I had found a life worth living on my own. I still wanted a partner someday but not with the soul-crushing desperation that sold dating books. However, the world at large and my mother, two groups of equal value, clearly could not accept this small degree of relaxation around my approach to dating.

To make it more complicated, my uterus hung over so many of my discussions about relationships. Did I want children? When would it happen? Why wasn't it happening? My ovaries got more acknowledgement than my goals or ambitions. But babies simply did not occur to me. When people discussed pregnancy, my thought process followed the trajectory of a to-do list. "Kids? Oh, you mean that thing where something comes out of you, and you put it through college…I've heard of it." I just kind of forgot. How does one forget to have kids? The same way one forgets to buy wasabi mayo at Trader Joe's—you just didn't want it that bad. But children, unlike condiments, should not be a "nice to have" but the product of visionary desire.

It's only through the grace of reproductive rights (and long dry spells supported by salsa) that eschewed a traditional life, which seemed wise considering how much ambivalence I felt. I believe passionately in what Ruth Bader Ginsberg describes as the "dignity" to choose to reproduce, rather than because of one's innate body parts. These rights, which—I can't even believe I am writing this—are under constant threat, are paramount to a woman's ability to create a life she loves. Not to mention, pregnancy can have serious consequences and result in health issues or even death. The United States has the highest maternal mortality rate in the developed world (Martin 2017). If men had to risk their lives to make a baby, we would be able to get abortions at the car wash vending machine.

While men, too, experience pressure to procreate, I can testify that a single woman not intent on a life centered around a family creates distress in those around her. This baffled me at first. The reason why anybody passes on having children—male or female—seems fairly obvious. Doing whatever you want, whenever you want, never gets old.

Without the question of children, I did not see the rush to find a life partner. As I continued to dance, I felt more peace with this decision, even if those around me did not. Even if I tired of salsa, which I did, maybe life afforded endless interest and adventures? Maybe, salsa wasn't the answer as an alternative to traditional marriage and monogamy. But, at the very least, salsa made single life not only more tolerable but preferable to a bad relationship. What salsa gave me was a community, a place to go, a tribe. Education freed me from the financial struggle that would make marriage an improvement on the quality of my life. But salsa freed me from isolation.

What to do when you are a feminine woman, but the traditional feminine roles of "wife" and "mother" feel like a crushing burden? When the institution of "marriage" fails to hold the requisite illusion? Salsa allowed me to fulfill the feminine archetype in the fantasy world created on the dance floor. I could put on my salsa shoes and pretend that I didn't need to work for money and forage for food at Trader Joe's. Salsa allowed me to be a delicate flower, an "egg." I dressed in heels and allowed a man to lead me. And then took the heels off and went to work and live the freedom of a first-world woman who has choices. A freedom, I might add, that I don't take for granted and that I give thanks for every day. Thank you, America. (For now.)

I have spoken to people in relationships who feel that a salsa dance satisfied their desire to deviate outside of their monogamous relationship. Salsa was a canvas, a place to project your fantasy, like Burning Man with far fewer white people. You could go to salsa and try out a new life, without destroying the current one.

Years later, Kim told me that she never regretted what she termed her "casual" phase. My friends with children adore their sons and daughters. I met a minister who performs ceremonies for any woman who wants to "marry" herself. It is nice to know that we have options.

Chapter 11
Salsa Abroad

Step 11: Dance in another country.

Dance is the hidden language of the soul, of the body.
—Martha Graham

To-Do List 3/7/2009

1. ~~Quit dysfunctional job~~
2. Turn thirty-seven
3. Go to Mexico and detox from Corporate America and excessive salsa dancing
4. Figure out the rest of your life
5. Maybe get pregnant?
6. Write a book
7. Put up some shelves in the bathroom
8. ~~Buy orchid food~~
9. Consider finding a "real" relationship

One day I stood on the promenade and gazed into the flurry of dancers moving in front of us. I felt disconnected from the music and the people, with no real desire to dance. Toddlers weaved in and out, their eyes glued to the giant humans before them.

It had been over three years since Lisa and I began this journey together into the heart of salsa.

"I think I need to take a break from salsa," I said to Lisa.

The night before found me in the backseat of an SUV two blocks from The Mayan at four o'clock in the morning. The Mayan, a large salsa club located in downtown LA, required patrons to pass through metal detectors.

I carpooled with two salsa chica friends to watch the finals of a salsa dance competition, won by a gay male couple. Afterward I sat in the backseat and waited while my two friends compared text messages and discussed the lies and half-truths of a salsa guy whose only connection to my life remained that his existence kept me from my bed.

"I think getting a certified therapist in the mix might be a good idea," I chimed in. "But I actually need to wake up early tomorrow."

"I'm so sorry you have to hear this," said The Girlfriend, as she turned around to look at me as if I were her child en route to soccer practice.

I had little patience for salsa drama on a good day. However, lately it seemed that salsa in general created less of a psychic switch. I was in a Slump.

The Salsa Slump shares similar characteristics with any slump: a lack of passion and a total intolerance for

SALSA CHICA

the less savory aspects of that activity. In salsa, this included the Sweaty Slime Hug, rough leads that threatened my rotator cuff, and the Salsa Drama, such as that played out by the two women in the car.

Historically, my Salsa Slumps preceded a rise to a new level of dancing. But this felt like total apathy, robotic motion, and disconnection, like I was dancing in a dream, or through murky water.

For three years, a night of dancing rewarded the work and drudgery of life. And then one day it stopped. All salsa dancers hit burnout. And at that point, many take a break or just stop.

Initially, salsa was a revolution, and the idea that I could dance my frustrations away, a revelation. In my first two years, I had thrown myself into an education that challenged my body and spirit. And it had been a labor of love.

Lisa and I had always pondered when the honeymoon would end.

"I keep thinking that someday, I'm just going to stop," she said to me once.

One day, I met a former Salsa Chica, Dorothy, for lunch and told her about my burnout and frustrations. "What are you doing hanging out with these guys?" she asked, as if she had been waiting for me to come to my senses.

After two years of dancing, Dorothy had concluded that the salsa scene was "not stimulating" and stopped cold. Dorothy, a bright and curious woman, enjoyed art openings, restaurants, and plays. But she also had recently lost her father and seemed to be in a different kind of slump. She confessed that she watched a lot more TV.

I needed a break. But I had a fear. Salsa put me in touch with something inside of me…the fire? The fear of losing that part of myself was greater than the loss of anything: job, guy, or even my youth. And no matter how disgusted I got by These Guys, the drama, the overplayed commercial music…no matter how much it all rankled my sense of myself as a dignified, respectable human being, I knew that a part of me still needed this.

Sometimes we need a change. And then we need to change again.

I spent my thirty-seventh birthday at the Warehouse. It fell on my last day as a digital producer at an advertising agency. My life had become a rigorous cycle of work, dance, sleep, work, dance, sleep…and then I hit a chronic level of fatigue. As my health deteriorated, I continued to show up at work where I dodged Nerf balls thrown by fraternity jocks who constituted the "creative team." Me and the lone female art director lamented how little agency culture had changed from that depicted on the TV show *Mad Men*, about a 1960s advertising agency in New York where female secretaries served the patriarchal white men. "I cannot feel any ironic detachment from that show," she said to me one day while we commiserated about the bro culture that placed us in the alternating roles of sex object, secretary or schoolmarm.

SALSA CHICA

In my blog, I wrote about work, with the assumption, crazy as it now seems, that nobody reads my blog. In one post, I wrote about the direction I received from a creative which consisted of, "make the web site really cool-looking." A few weeks later, my boss sat down beside me and said, "everyone knows about the blog." I sat there in a shocked mortification. She kindly asked me to "take the post down." Then she laughed. Because no woman enjoys an office run by misogynist bros.

At night I danced because I needed salsa to repair the spiritual damage of a sexist and toxic work environment. Without the physical and creative outlet of salsa I felt like a shadow of a human being.

"Leaving the country is the only way I can stop working or salsa dancing," I told Lisa one night at the Warehouse.

At some point in the night Ernie, a rotund fiftyish Mexican, one of my first dance partners at Casa Escobar, took me aside. He told a friend that he believed in aliens and that once twenty beautiful women stood in line to dance with him. But he was always kind to me, and I felt fond of him.

"You have changed since I've known you," he said. "You have become more beautiful."

"Thank you" I said, sincerely touched.

"You are very pretty, for thirty-seven," he said.

Maybe something was lost in translation, but I choose to believe that he meant "for thirty-seven" as in "a woman way over her prime."

"I want you to listen to me," he continued. In the background the DJ sang a romantic song into the mic and did not sound bad. "You are very special person. You need to find a good guy. Not one of these guys who has no respect for women."

"I have heard this before," I replied.

"She is my favorite," he told a man beside us.

"*Todo el mundo es su favorita*," said the man. (This translates to "Everyone is your favorite.")

A week later, I arrived in San Miguel de Allende, a Mexican city near Guanajuato with a large expatriate American retirement community. I knew not a single person. I made the decision to go after a coworker posted pictures of the city on Facebook.

I love Mexico. As a child, my mother and I visited Mexico every summer after she separated from my father. We traveled to Guanajuato, Oaxaca, Vera Cruz, and Puerto Vallarta. We wandered around museums and plazas, risked our digestive systems on street food, and talked to street vendors. One time we met a weaver on the bus who invited us to her home to look at her loom. In those days, my mom was a free spirit.

For the first few days, I spent a lot of time alone. I sat in the *centro* by myself, with coffee or ice cream, and tried to just "be." It had been so long since I had sat still. I wanted to run off and find somewhere to dance. In fact, I struggled through a serious case of Salsa Withdrawals, especially at night.

SALSA CHICA

I watched the tourists, families, and couples. More than a few retired sixty-plus men tried to pick me up.

I soon met the local salsa dance teacher who gave me the lowdown on the salsa scene, and, in time, I connected with the entire miniscule salsa scene. Salsa friends had told me that whenever they travelled, in any part of the world, they found salsa dancers. Which makes sense, as the LA salsa scene consists of dancers from Japan, Israel, Mexico, Columbia, France, China, and Holland. Wherever one or more dancers gathered with a speaker and a smart phone, a salsa scene was born. In this sense, salsa is almost like a universal culture, a worldwide language, or a cult.

I wanted to meet the local dancers, but I needed to sit still in my skin without rushing off. What was I running from?

I had spent three (sort of) prime childbearing years on the dance floor and, while I sat in the centro and watched families I contemplated the nature of people connected through biology, chained to each other. Was this what I wanted?

Salsa felt like my chain, albeit a loose, sort of long, dangly necklace. But who said all chains have to be chokers? Would I have fared better if I had dated on the internet in search of a relationship "as if it were a job" and focused on my biological clock like a project?

Dancing had been the bridge that brought me closer to a sense of my body and myself. Salsa was the one area in my life in which I had absolutely followed my own beat, without judgment, reservation, or boundaries. I danced to my heart's desire and my body's limit. I had been led to many new and exciting places, in life and in myself. Salsa had brought me friends, a sense of community, connection to my body, and a way to express myself without words or my brain. Salsa loved me back.

I met the majority of salsa dancers by teaching a ladies' styling class at the one salsa club, Mama Mia, and became friends with a veterinarian named Maria. She was in love with her coworker, a fellow vet and salsa dancer, who told her about his flings.

"I know he doesn't love them," she told me.

"We call them 'booty calls,'" I explained.

"He doesn't want a girlfriend," she added.

"He sounds like a salsero," I continued, as I recalled my night in the SUV, where a similar conversation took place. My own innate protection of women thrust me in the role of wise older sister to single salsa women everywhere. "Boy, it doesn't matter how big or small the salsa scene is," I told her. "There's salsa drama everywhere."

One night Maria and I went to the karaoke club and sang the song "Un Montón de Estrellas" (A Mountain of Stars) by Gilberto Santa Rosa about a man who can't let go of a relationship to a woman he loves.

Porque yo en el amor
soy un idiota
Translated:
Because in love
I am a moron

SALSA CHICA

I always thought of romantic love as a girly thing, but Gilberto Santa Rosa, a royal figure of Salsa Romantica, proved me wrong. Love turned Gilberto into an idiot. It made him human.

Maybe my single life, a big experiment in the context of history, was not a miserable failure, but the trial that I needed.

I felt proud of my ability to travel alone. Maybe I could have more experiences, try new things, and appreciate the gift of health and strength.

For the rest of the trip, I woke up late, wandered into town, shopped for gifts, took myself out to dinner, and photographed the lovely town. Two young guys, who liked to prey on female tourists, as Maria later explained, "befriended" me. By the end of the trip, I hid from them when I walked through town.

When I got home, Lisa described me as "glowing." The Salsa Slump, for the time being, had ended.

I planned to look for another job. But in 2009, the economy tanked, and I remained unemployed for months to come. So I just kept dancing.

Chapter 12
La Palabra (The Word)

Step 12: Listen to salsa lyrics.

It is, of course, possible to dance a prayer.
—Glade Byron Adams

Salsa on the Third Street Promenade in Santa Monica, 2019

SOLANGE CASTRO

One summer day in 2009, the DJ on the promenade played "Rebelión (No Le Pegue a la Negra)," a classic song often performed by salsa bands at clubs all over Los Angeles. I overheard my friend, Sarah, sing, "Don't hit my black woman," to the tune of the song.

"That's what the lyrics say," she explained. "'No pegue a la negra' translates to 'Don't hit my black woman.'"

While I had danced to the song dozens of times, I never realized that the lyrics told the story of a black slave in Cartagena, Colombia in the 1600s who defends his wife against a slave master. In my quest to find dance partners, nail my moves, and keep my wardrobe malfunctions under control, I failed to notice that the pain of slavery had traveled from Cartagena hundreds of years ago to twenty-first century Santa Monica.

The lyrics in Spanish read:

Un matrimonio africano, esclavos de
Un español, él les daba muy mal trato
Y a su negra le pegó
Y fue alli, se revelo el negro guapo, tomó
Venganza por su amor y aún se escucha
En la verja, no le pegue a mi negra
No le pegue a la negra

This translates to:

An African couple, slaves of a Spaniard
He treated them very badly

SALSA CHICA

And hit his black woman
It was then, that the heroic black man rebelled
He avenged his love
And you can still hear him yelling at the gates:
Don't hit my black woman

Once I understood the lyrics to "Rebelión" I began to study the lyrics of other salsa songs. Salsa cover bands tend to play the same songs, many of which are classics that have possibly survived centuries. I am far from an expert or a historian, but I realized that many salsa songs were ballads, stories about major social and life events in Latin American countries. Many range in topics from love to tragedy.

"El Cuarto de Tula" is about a fire that kills a beautiful, young, single woman named Tula after she falls asleep with a lit candle in her room. It follows various local characters as the fire spreads throughout the city. Several versions of the same song exist, and most use similar music but different lyrics. In another version, the lyrics describe the search for firemen to put out the fire. Yet another version focuses on the tragedy of this single woman dying alone. In this sense, salsa really is about the "fire!" Not to mention the anxiety created by a single woman living alone.

A lot of salsa music touches on the hardships of life. "Calle Luna, Calle Sol" describes a dangerous neighborhood where residents contend with robbery and murder. "La Malanga" is about an African vegetable that fails to grow and the consequent starvation that ensues. Some salsa songs focus on silly stuff like "La Pelota," which, as far as I can tell, is about a mom who wishes her son would quit playing soccer. "A Comer Chicharrón," translates to "Eating Fried Pork Skins." Racial injustice, poverty, and fried food: this is the stuff of salsa.

Willie Colon's "El Gran Varon" tells the story of a father who rejects his gay, transgendered son, who later dies alone of AIDS in a hospital. Can you dance and cry at the same time? Salsa seems to think so.

Unlike commercial hip-hop songs, I rarely hear salsa songs about gangsters, money, and men and their "bitches." One exception is a classic, "Mala Mujer" (Bad Woman) by La Sonora Matancera, about a heartless woman who the singer/song writer believes "no tiene corazon." The lyrics "mata la," loosely translate to "kill her!" A more literal translation might be "kill the hoe."

Little do many non-Spanish speakers know that they are moving to a beat that tells the story of hardship, human suffering, or a pre-dinner snack. But perhaps the power of the music comes from the underlying expression of joy in the face of human suffering. Without conscious awareness, the music spoke to my own personal sense of triumph against trauma and disappointment. Salsa is redemption in the face of life's tribulations. Salsa says, "A shit storm hit, but we're still here."

Outside of the lyrics, the music has its own tradition. According to Tijana Ilich's "What is Salsa Music and What Is Its Origin?" many salsa songs follow the call-and-response patterns of traditional African songs and then break into the chorus (Ilich 2018).

The origins of salsa remain unclear. Between 1930 and 1960, musicians from Cuba, Puerto Rico, Mexico, and South America came to New York to perform. As they listened to each other, their native rhythms and forms fused and evolved, creating mambo, jazz, cha-cha, and what we call "salsa."

Salsa fuses sounds from many countries and continents, including classical music. Ricardo Ray's and Bobby Cruz's, "Sonido Bestial" includes Ray's solo of Chopin's Etude Op. 10, No. 12. "Sonido Bestial," possibly my favorite song of all time (yes, even beating Prince's "Purple Rain"), means "bestial sound."

One bright summer Sunday, I watched the dancers on the promenade when the DJ played a medium tempo cha-cha.

"What is the name of this song?" I asked Angel.

"Ritmo con ashé," he replied.

"Ritmo con what?" I knew that "ritmo" means rhythm.

"Ashé."

"What does that mean?"

"It means, like, your power. It's an African word."

Ashé is, actually, a Yoruban word meaning "divine life force." It comes from the religion of Santería, brought to the Caribbean along with kidnapped slaves. What is the English equivalent of "ashé?" I don't think it exists. "Inner power" doesn't cut it, "the force" isn't in the dictionary, and I don't think "mojo" is a real word.

SOLANGE CASTRO

Along with their culture and language, the Yorubans also brought their drumming practices. The drum rhythms were meant to call forth various gods and spirits who offer guidance. Many of these rhythms found their way into Cuban music, and, ultimately, are a part of much of what we call salsa today. My friend Diana, an African drummer, says that the drum is the closest instrument to the beat of the heart.

Many famous salsa singers like Celia Cruz and Héctor Lavoe embraced the religion of Santeria. The Yoruban faith believes in "Orishas," individual-specific spirits, who provide direct guidance. Each person has a specific Orisha, who offers a way to understand his or her individual place in the universe. Celia Cruz dedicated an album to Orishas called "Tributo a Los Orishas." She, like many salsa musicians, accessed her spirituality through dance, drum, and song. So, to call "salsa" a religion is not really an exaggeration.

I never understood the powerful drive I felt to be around salsa music. I chalked it up to a desire to meet men and dance. But the more I danced, the more I believed that the music drove me to dance.

Celia Cruz wrote many lyrics. One song, "Yo Viviré," is a salsa-fied version of Gloria Gaynor's hit, "I Will Survive." However, "Yo Viviré" has nothing to do with a loser guy who bails but focuses on how her own musical legacy will, indeed, live on. The lyrics celebrate how her "voice" will continue in the soul of her people, and the feet of the dancers who move to her music. "I will live" sounds a lot better than "I will survive," and Celia Cruz, who gained twenty-three gold albums in her career, received a star on the Walk of Fame in Hollywood, and the National Medal of Arts in 1994, indeed lives on as The Queen of Salsa Music. She also, by the way, never married or had children.

Chapter 13
Salsa Boundaries

Step 13: Learn to say "no."

Next time you're mad, try dancing out your anger.
—Sweetpea Tyler

Salsa taught me a behavior that, in retrospect, I needed to learn. Some might call it "boundaries." Or the ability to say "No." Or even "Hell no," when necessary. In the excessively physical, touchy-feely, huggy, and what some might consider "inappropriate" touching of strangers, I learned how to say "No" to aggressive, creepy or just misguided human interactions. I learned to say "No" to dances, touch, or close contact with certain people. You might learn this in childhood or in therapy. I learned it on the dance floor.

While I approached salsa like a little girl set loose at Disneyland, I had enough street smarts to remain aware of the seedier elements of an activity that often takes place around alcohol. The dark side of salsa reflects the worst part of society. Lurkers who stare at girls; intoxicated dancers who harass, assault, or just give a rough lead; teachers who assault students; and the general ethos of addiction that pervade an activity often lumped into "partying."

Even with my awareness, I had my fair share of violations to confront. One time Ruben put his hand on my butt and squeezed. I asked him to stop in a far too polite tone of voice, to which he replied, "I'm just playing with you." I reasoned that he had been drinking and "it's no big deal" or whatever else I needed to tell myself to shove down the anger that surfaced. I still felt grateful to him for teaching me to dance when I knew nothing, for the nights when he pulled me out of the corner like Patrick Swayze or listened to my complaints. He seemed to care. But his behavior on this night fell into the category of "unacceptable" and definitely "Not OK." My gratitude for his better qualities leads me to dance with him today. But he will not grab my butt again.

I had other challenges. One night, while at Mor Bar, I sat down to rest when a sometimes dance partner named Ethan sat down beside me and put his arm around me. A successful attorney, Ethan belonged to the category of white salseros who, despite their genetic make-up, had developed a decent lead. Although he treated salsa like an investment portfolio, Ethan could, actually, hold the beat quite well.

However, I never signed up to have his arm around me off the dance floor. I wondered when he would move it. I wasn't sure why he felt entitled to put it there and

SALSA CHICA

did not feel good about how it signified some relationship between us…but as in so many instances, I accepted it as due course, payment even, for the privilege to do this sacred, wonderful thing. Besides, what was so godawful about being pawed once in a while? As Lisa would say, "Chica, it's Salsa World," before she leaped into the arms of an unsuspecting victim who may or may not have enjoyed catching a white lady.

Then Ethan said the following: "Do girls get hot and sticky down there the way guys do?"

I tried to ignore the question.

"Are you shy? Are you a shy-gina?"

I might have gotten up and walked away. I don't remember. I felt disgusted. I spoke about it to some female friends, but most held Lisa's attitude. "Oh, it's salsa world," they said.

I already sensed a disturbing side to Ethan's personality. I rarely found salsa dancers to be aggressive. Either salseros are a less angry breed, or salsa music has a soothing effect on anger or testosterone. In all my years, I only saw one fight in a salsa club, but it ended in eight counts.

When I first started to learn salsa, I felt surprised by the nonchalance with which any salsa guy might treat a momentary physical injury, especially one that I inflicted on him. I might whack him in the head, but most guys just shrugged it off with a "forget about it," as if it were due course, which it often was. But whenever anyone bumped into Ethan, he would stop and mutter something like "fucking asshole," as if he had just been violated in the deepest and most personal way. His expression reminded me of Sam Eagle from The Muppets.

However, Ethan always complimented my "beautiful style," and, in those days, before I went cold turkey on compliments, flattery remained the crack cocaine of my self-esteem. So, despite his socially inappropriate comments, I tolerated Ethan for his lead and honeyed words and, most importantly, because I am conflict avoidant and, on some level, he scared me.

The next time he asked me to dance, I said, "No thank you." As you might guess, this did not go over well. Ethan, suddenly, went from being a mildly annoying pursuer to a scary stalker. I must have given him my Vistaprint business card because he had my number, and calls, texts, and emails filled my phone. I ignored his messages. Maybe it would just blow over?

No such luck. One night he approached me.

"How dare you not respond to my email!" he yelled so loud he almost drowned out the live band.

I did not know what to do. I had been able to take care of most unwanted interactions in salsa with a nonverbal cue. The old Refusal to Make Eye Contact usually sufficed to ward off unwanted dance requests and other offers.

"Please don't yell at me," I said as gracefully as possible and walked away. A few minutes later he was in front of me…yelling again. Salsa music played in the background and people danced, as Ethan raged. I might

SALSA CHICA

have found it comical if the words "restraining order" had not also come to mind. I began to fear that my physical well-being was in danger. What if he was a complete lunatic? Or a Jeffrey Dahmer type? Would my head end up in his trunk? I managed to slink away and later asked Lisa to drive me to my car.

"Chica, just respond to his email and say, 'I'm sorry if I hurt your feelings' and leave it at that.'"

I went home and did just that. By early the next morning, he had already emailed me.

A chill ran down my spine. He was not going to leave me alone. Of all the men that parked themselves in Salsa World, the one to actually instill fear in me was a white, mustached lawyer who made well over a six-figure income and owned a home in Culver City.

"These guys are all the lowlifes and thugs in society," Lisa said once.

I begged to differ, but at least the so-called "lowlifes and thugs" respected my nonverbal avoidant cues.

I stayed away from Ethan for the next few months. Whenever I saw him, I felt knives shoot out of his eyes at me.

"Why don't you just tell him off?" offered Angel when I confided in him. And then he looked me in the eye. "Never mind," he added. "You're not capable of it."

When Angel had told me that my salsa needed to be "angrier and more aggressive" or that I didn't have "the fire," he spoke to my inability to assert myself against the Ethans of this world.

In time, I learned that it wasn't just me, of course. Ethan gained a reputation as a "stalker" and general creep. But in my interaction with him, I saw my inability to really stand up for myself. I had wilted in fear, not demanded that he leave me alone with the completely appropriate "Hell no, motherfucker" level of boundary. As a professional, he would have respected that. Something inside of me allowed myself to get bullied by this mediocre salsa dancer.

But my lack of gangster boundaries was only part of the problem. Ethan was not the only man I met who had a problem with the word "no."

I saw again and again how men in salsa, much like the world, felt entitled to women's bodies. It's not just the culture of salsa that adheres to the belief that while men can behave in ways that challenge the moral compass of Harvey Weinstein, and still earn money and find supporters, a woman can and should be punished for even the perceived offense of rejection. That "no" can be to sex, procreation, touch, or, in my case, a dance.

"That girl said 'no' to me three times," said a salsa dancer to me one night. "I'm never asking her to dance again. She's a fucking bitch."

"I never say 'no' to guys," said my friend Rebecca, a twenty-year-old student. "If you say no too much, you'll get blacklisted at Steven's Steakhouse. You don't want that reputation at a place like that."

Another young dancer, Roseanne, a hairdresser from Sweden, told me that Relentless warned her not to say

SALSA CHICA

"no" to guys for the same reason. Of course, he never fed me that line.

One time I said "no" to a man and then danced with someone else. While I was within my rights, this is also considered bad dance etiquette. The original man then yelled in my face, "You're a bad person!" What made me a bad person? Not wanting a total stranger to touch my body? Was I the Mother Theresa of salsa dances? I once read an article about clubs in New York in which working-class men paid women to dance with them. Shoot, I thought, I've been doing this for free.

In time, after years in salsa, I and most women I knew came around to the lesson that all people learn: we all have a right to our own bodies. Especially when it comes to who touches it and how.

However, I do try to respect the feelings of humans in general. As a writer and performer, I have experienced my share of rejection. Nobody needs it shoved in his or her face.

In the beginning, I rarely just said "No, thank you" but gave a list of excuses. These might include:

1. The song is too fast.
2. I'm resting.
3. I'm tired (which is different from "I'm resting" because it implies that I'm close to done).

Now I say "no" whenever I want. Let them fume, if they must. I am also allowed to change my mind. There are no rules. But like with the reflexes that allow me to follow and catch anything thrown at me, salsa improved my awareness of my desires, instincts, and ability to assess a situation in the moment. I will forever make mistakes and perhaps find myself in dances, relationships, or work situations where the thought dawns on me, "I don't want to be here." But I always have a choice.

A few months later, Ethan approached me at Monsoon one night and extended his hand. He made no apology or explanation but gave me a pleading look.

"No, thank you," I said. I just stared at him. I saw a middle-aged, white guy with crippling insecurity.

"I'm offering you my hand," he added. I didn't know what that meant, but it was not an apology.

"No," I repeated. I felt a little sorry for him. Which is why I didn't say, "Hell no, motherfucker." That would have been rude.

Chapter 14
Todo Tiene Su Final (Everything Comes to an End)

Step 14: Grieve.

...learn to dance with the limp.
—Anne Lamott

Me and mom, 1973

After six years of dancing, my attendance at salsa fluctuated with the seasons. And then I got into a relationship with a non-salsa dancer for three years. He liked to take long walks and run on the beach but did not dance. He did not mind if I went. However, I sometimes felt uncomfortable. Salsa felt like an ex you might have coffee with. It was kind of cheating.

But I still went to the Third Street Promenade on most Sundays, along with a growing population of new dancers as well as old-timer salseros, like Relentless, Angel, Ruben, Lisa, and dozens of friends. Carl, a tall, white man, stood outside for six hours with a boombox. The Sunday promenade salsa scene calls itself the Salsa Familia (the Salsa Family). If family is where you end up when you have nowhere else to be, the name fits.

In the winters, the Sunday salsa scene shrinks with people reticent to dance in the cold, but over the years Carl and his boombox have become increasingly resilient to the weather, and neither rain, wind, nor cold will deter those in search of a salsa fix. It feels good to dance to stay warm, sweat out the week, and see friends who have known you for years. And it feels really good to have somewhere to go when your life upends completely. Which is what happened in 2015 when my mother died.

I once fought with my mom over whether we should watch *Step Up Revolution*. She argued that it was worth two hours of terrible acting because "it has dancing." Anything with "dancing" was worth watching. Knowing what I know today, I would gladly sit through *Step Up*

SALSA CHICA

2: The Streets with her a thousand times. Like most Americans obsessed with age-defying eye cream, I never really thought about how it would all end, for me or anyone. Nobody talked to me about death. If my parents did mention death, its purpose was to manipulate me into coming home for Christmas.

Whenever I heard Hector Lavoe's classic salsa song, "Todo Tiene Su Final" (Everything Comes to an End), I assumed he sang about the fragility of romantic love or the last call for alcohol.

Todo tiene su final, nada dura para siempre
Tenemos que recordar que no existe eternidad

This translates to:

Everything comes to an end, nothing lasts forever
We need to remember that eternity doesn't exist.

Love ends, the bar closes, the DJ packs it up, and if you don't get to the valet in time, he will leave your car keys on the curb. But after my mother died, the meaning of the song changed for me in a profound paradigm shift. Now I realize that he was not singing about the last call for alcohol, but the finality of death. The song is a not-so-gentle reminder that we will not live forever. We only have today.

When I accepted this, I never regretted the late nights spent dancing in bliss. When I danced, I felt alive. And when my mother died, I realized that someday I will too.

After my mother found out she had stage IV ovarian cancer, the oncologist, aka The Angel of Death, made it plain that she would "die of this disease." I have had many terrible jobs, but no occupation rates worse than that of an oncologist. For a time, my mother struggled through the treatment but still had periods of normality. But when that time ended, she suffered. It was unbearable to watch. Death seemed like a relief.

I read a book written by hospice workers that painted death as a special time, an opening between earth and the afterlife. I expected nothing less than an apparition of my grandmother and maybe some flashes of light. The reality proved more grizzly and real.

When she finally passed, I felt tremendous relief. She would no longer suffer. But I had no idea of the future to come. She will never see this book. She will never see me do anything again. For the first few months, it felt like she had gone on a trip. Life went on with shocking normality.

And then came reality. I distracted myself to both avoid and face grief, a giant chasm that appeared and disappeared at random in the years that followed.

For a period of time right before and then after my mother died, I could not dance. I tried. I showed up, but I could not feel anything. It did not matter the song, the partner, or even my desire to want to feel salsa. It went beyond a salsa slump. The spirit that drove me to dance lay dormant, disinterested, and kind of bored. I stood and watched everyone else, lost in the music and endorphins,

SALSA CHICA

and free from the burden of sadness. I wanted to be a part of it. It looked like fun. But I did not feel moved. I stood outside the life force, a person in grief.

It occurred to me that my desire to dance always felt like a way to celebrate my life. That dancing itself is a celebration. But after my mother's illness and death, the pendulum of life swung in the opposite direction. Grief asks for quiet, stillness and solitude.

Like many people who lose someone close, I found that the mention of death made social interactions awkward. I could not even say the word "dead" in public. She "passed," "transitioned," or "departed." I felt like a plague on people's happiness. Who wants to hear that you spent a night crying into a pillow? I needed to share my dreams about her and about how one night, after a bad dream, the lamp she bought me mysteriously flashed on. (Or I thought it did.) Despite the inevitability of it for every single person, I found few who tolerated the discussion. Those tended to be people who have also lost a parent or loved one.

A year after she died, my boyfriend broke up with me. This was also the year that Donald Trump was elected. In January of 2017, I felt that life could not get worse. Then I found a lump in my breast and realized that life can always get worse. The lump was just a cyst, so my life did not get worse but just remained in the same shitty place. Some days I could not get out of bed. I woke up to start a regiment of crying, and I went to bed to the relief of a Netflix binge. I watched terrible shows and anything about the zombie apocalypse. The end of the world felt right.

While I did not feel like dancing at all, I returned to the promenade and to occasional parties and events because I knew the friendship, music, and stimulation would help me out of an isolation that felt oddly comfortable. My salsa friends, many of whom I had known over a decade, welcomed me.

The first year after my mother died, my salsa friends insisted that I participate in the tradition of a "Birthday Dance" wherein partners of the birthday person dance with him or her in a circle. In my heyday, Ruben and the Ninjas dragged me across the floor and threw me in the air. Out of salsa shape, I prayed that I would survive without a major concussive injury.

But often I just listened to the music. It did not seep into my soul or inspire me to move, but it still felt better to stand there and watch, to know that life could be fun in theory, if not for me.

My friends saw me as the same person I had always been. But I wasn't. I was no longer a daughter of a mother. Everything had changed, and I did not know who I was in this new mother-less world.

Through dance I rebelled against my mom. Salsa allowed me to assert myself as a body separate from hers. Now that she was gone, I was free but alone, broken off from the love she gave me. In a sense, I did not need to dance the way I did when she told me to take vitamins and demanded I have children or find an old, rich, bald man to marry. I did not need to rebel because there was no longer anyone to rebel against. Such is the burden of losing your parents. It's dancing with a ghost.

One night, after my mother's "passing," I forced myself to go to Wokcano, an Asian fusion restaurant, which hosted an outdoor dance floor. I danced a few times but mostly stood around and talked to friends, watched younger dancers, and marveled at their fresh salsa glow.

My old friend Ernie approached me. Still rotund, he hardly moved when he danced. But he still enjoyed it.

"Nunca te veo," he said. (I never see you.)

"I don't go out very much anymore," I said. "I just don't feel like it."

"A veces la salsa luz se apaga," he said. (Sometimes the salsa light goes out).

That sounded about right. My salsa light had burned out. I was just a lamp with an expired bulb.

I worried I would never emerge from the darkness. How could I screw in a new light bulb to the lamp of my soul?

I no longer could feel salsa. But I still wanted to dance. One summer day a few months after my mother died, I sat at home, on unemployment and overwhelmed by grief. Something told me to look for a dance class at Santa Monica College (SMC). I saw on the schedule that the deadline to sign up for the class was thirty minutes away. I pulled on my yoga pants and rushed to SMC. I risked a parking ticket and arrived to class seconds before the teacher handed out the final code I needed to sign up. The jazz dance teacher, Angela, choreographed deep soulful dances that led me out of my grief that semester. Surrounded by nineteen- and twenty-year-old women, I lost myself in choreography to Sam Smith, Adelle, and Ed Sheeran. I came home each night after class transformed.

Her class helped me get through all the weird death markers: memorial organization, headstone purchase, and paperwork and a series of life mishaps that plagued me the year after she died, including an abscessed tooth, bird mites, and even mice. It was like the universe (colloquial LA speak for "God") was trying to get my attention. That is, if the universe is sadist.

Flashes of life came and went. In a few years, I met a new guy and worked on a cool project. Then I lost the guy, and the project ended. I never had stability with work before my mother died, but without her around to stress about it with me, I felt unmoored. It was so easy to feel sorry for myself. I could no longer lean on her or rely on her to share my troubles. It felt like the very foundation of the ground had given away and each step forward made me trip and fall.

On most days, I convinced myself that a night at home with my anxiety and Netflix would restore me. But stress and isolation make poor friends, and *Stranger Things* just wasn't cutting it. One day in 2018, three years after my mother's "departure," a few dancers hosted a summer salsa party at a condo located about half a mile from my apartment.

A friend suggested that I go to the party and dance

SALSA CHICA

as much as I could physically tolerate. She said I needed a shot of endorphins. It seemed strange that I needed such advice, as I had spent years on a schedule structured around a "fuck everything and dance" mentality. But my grief erased past joys. I was starting life over.

The invite to the party, held in the community area of a condo, encouraged guests to use the swimming pool. I put on a bathing suit and shorts and walked over to the party at three o'clock in the afternoon.

I walked into a large mostly empty hall with a few couples on the dance floor. Someone set out a punch bowl of jungle juice. I downed a cup of liquid the color of red Kool-Aid, which tasted like twenty kinds of alcohol. A dance partner grabbed me just as the jungle juice concoction kicked in, and before I could judge the music or bikini-clad dancers on the floor, my inner Lady Who Can't Get off the Dance Floor switch turned on. In truth, Lady Who Can't Get off the Dance Floor had existed pre-salsa and appeared at weddings. But in the years since my mother passed, she had fallen asleep.

After the song ended, I danced again, drank more jungle juice, danced, drank, rinse, repeat. I danced for two hours, in a large hall with no air-conditioning. My hair dripped with sweat, which flew off my body like a rotating sprinkler when I spun. Worry, loss, and depression seemed like memories from another life. At a certain point, I felt so overheated that I ran outside, took off my shorts, and jumped into the pool. I dried off and then went back onto the dance floor for another few hours. Mascara dripped down my face, and my hair dried into a chlorinated pile of frizz. The floor became soaked with water and dirt. I no longer cared.

Lisa came later and took one look at me and said, "You look great."

"Must. Keep. Dancing."

I had allowed a crack of light to shine in. Don't ever underestimate salsa, jungle juice, or condo pools in Marina Del Rey. My problems awaited me the next day. But I had taken a break from the weight of the darker parts of life, grief, fear and anxiety.

And that was the first time since my mother died that I remembered what salsa felt like. The first time since her passing that I felt alive.

Chapter 15
Forever Salsa Chica

Step 15: Dance, dance, dance.

There are short-cuts to happiness, and dancing is one of them.

—Vicki Baum

Dancing with Raul at a summer salsa party, 2018

People sometimes ask me, "Why salsa?" While I can postulate that I am Latinx and like to dance, I admit that I don't have a great answer. I know people who tried salsa and felt "meh" about it but then thrived in swing, tango, beach volleyball, knitting, or Aikido. Why does anyone fall in love with any kind of activity or art form? Based on my own experience, sometimes the reason for that helpless desire is a mystery even to oneself. But I do believe that finding what some refer to as "your thing" can change a life. When I drive by a concert venue on Sunset Boulevard and see a bunch of kids in the same accoutrements, piercings and black T-shirts, I understand that they are nourishing their souls. Despite appearances, people rushing out to practice Krav Maga or play Horror Trivia or "yes and" at improv are healthy and alive. Salsa just happened to be my path, the subculture activity that unplugged me from the matrix, and in the end, that is all that matters.

When I think about those early years, when I spun out of control and idolized the Ninjas, bought a gold-sequined dress, or drove home at one o'clock on a Thursday morning all I remember is the warmth in my body, and the glow in my soul.

Despite how my mother felt about my salsa dancing, my years in salsa no longer seemed like an odd, tangential path but the one time in my whole life when I followed my heart and "lived" in the moment, without thinking about how I looked, the future, the past, or personal gain. My drive to dance felt pure.

SALSA CHICA

Dancing helped me in ways that went beyond my body. I credit the hours spent on the dance floor with creative output. Four years into salsa, I wrote a play about dating in Los Angeles. A few years later I produced the play, "Changes in The Mating Strategies of White People," and it ran for six weeks. One night, while in my "salsa slump," I wrote a joke. I went to an open mic to try it out and, thus, re-launched a standup comedy vocation that began in my twenties.

My salsa life seemed foreign to my comedy friends. I spoke about it on Jackie Kashan's *Dork Forest* podcast and gave Maria Bamford a lesson for my sporadic one-minute web series, "Teaching Comics to Dance Salsa."

Through my web series and by offering private lessons, I discovered how terrified most people feel to inhabit their bodies through dance. The act of dance induces terror, dread, and anxiety for many, mostly Caucasian, people.

White Americans remain a minority in the mostly Latinx, Asian, African American, and European community of salsa in Los Angeles. Most non-American cultures come from some kind of dancing tradition. However, white Americans seem the least inclined to dance. I met a man recently, born in the fifties, who lamented all the concerts he attended where he simply sat and watched.

"I loved the Rolling Stones and the Who. The music was amazing," he said. "But we just sat and watched. I now think that's sad."

Stories like his lead me to believe in the importance of a dance community in a person's life. However, life pulled me in other directions. While I continued to show up to socials and the promenade, I performed in comedy shows, started a podcast, joined a yoga studio, and my nights of leaving my house at ten o'clock at night and staying out till two o'clock in the morning receded into the past. The salsa community also shifted and changed; new dancers came in and became star teachers; and older salsa dancers left town or found other careers. Some of my friends married, had children, switched to tango or west coast swing, earned PhDs, traveled, or relocated. I went to weddings, held salsa babies, and danced with new young dancers who blossomed seemingly overnight.

On a recent day, a friend asked if I could teach salsa dancing to kids at a church summer camp. When I asked the kids to break out into a line of followers and leaders, most of the girls went to the leader line, and the boys went to the follower line. I showed them the step for each group and asked them to find a partner from the opposite line.

"Wait, aren't they doing the boys' part?" asked one boy.

"That's what a leader does," I explained. "What we call the 'boys' part,' but we don't have rules here."

At this point, he and some of the male followers switched to the leader line.

"OK, now everyone finds a partner," I said.

SALSA CHICA

Everyone chose a same-sex partner. That is, except for my partner, Dustin.

In a matter of minutes, Dustin had the footwork down and incorporated his own upper body moves. His "flavor." According to my friend, Dustin had a rough time fitting in at the camp. And then came salsa. Dustin is a dancer.

Other kids struggled, and one looked like he had just been locked onto a roller coaster and could not get out.

"How did that feel?" I asked after we practiced the steps to music.

"I was so scared I thought I was going to throw up!" shouted one kid. "But then it got really fun!"

Whenever I teach salsa, whether to children or adults, I am witness to a storm of emotions: panic, frustration, excitement, and then joy. If I were queen of the world, I would demand that all children and teens study some form of partner dance.

I feel so lucky to have this superpower, as a friend once described it. The psychological, mental and emotional benefits have hardly been championed in our big-screen society.

In a study at the Albert Einstein College of Medicine, researchers found that dancing improved mental acuity and decreased dementia by 76 percent. Far more than swimming or bicycling (0 percent), or doing crossword puzzles (47 percent) (Powers 2010). Social dancing, which involves split-second decision making, creates new neural pathways and improves white matter.

Especially in the learning stage. Followers gain the most from the cerebral benefits of dancing because they must make hundreds of split-second decisions. I can attest that dancing gave me greater spatial cognition, helped me develop awareness of my body and gave me faster reflexes. While all partner dances offer benefits, followers develop the greatest agility. As Ginger Rogers famously said, she did everything Fred Astaire did "but backwards and in heels."

On most Sundays I dance on the promenade. While still my favorite venue, nothing about the promenade is ideal for dancing. The concrete floor skews at an angle, making it hard to balance. The battery for the boombox often dies mid-song, and everyone stands around and waits for the management to fix it. Often, it comes back to life through magic or a few bangs. Salseros bring their instruments and backup the clave beat, which often results in at least one horrible off-beat clanging that I try to ignore. But dancing outside on a Sunday remains the perfect Sunday night ritual. The only religion I ever practiced with consistency.

For a few years, Lisa disappeared. She had foot surgery and feared she might never dance again.

However, in time, she returned, albeit in flatter shoes. In her sixties, she still keeps up with the twenty-five-year-olds.

"Chica, I still got some years left in me."

I see Relentless, who always makes sure to give me a big, inappropriate hug. Sometimes I get a nod from

SALSA CHICA

Angel, who has a new, blond girlfriend and then another, and I dance with Ruben, who has a a son. I never see Guillermo, but based on social media, I trust he has found happiness. Every Sunday somebody has a birthday dance, and some tourist or passerby will ask me, "How do you learn?" as if I am an ambassador of salsa. Having written a book about it, it's fair to say that I am.

I dance in the rain, the cold, and the heat and amid tourists, toddlers, creepy guys who take videos (please stop), and whoever else stands and observes this strange and wondrous activity. Through my mother's death, breakups, unemployment, general depression, sadness, Trump's election, PMS, and all my fears and anxieties about money and relationships, I return to the promenade every Sunday and to something inside of myself. Sometimes I just talk to friends or listen to Lisa tell me about her latest Bumble date. She still likes younger men and vodka, but salsa in her words "is the best thing I ever did."

Sometimes I just watch. And, once in a while, a partner will show up, a hardcore On 2 dancer, and everything recedes, time stops, the earth drops away, and I lose ten years of stress. I feel rejuvenated and able to face life again. Other days I go home, salsa checked off on my to-do list.

I marvel at the diversity of the group. In what other community do people of Latino, Korean, Chinese, Japanese, Israeli, Persian, Dutch, Jewish, and African American descent, as well as of every religious and political leaning (best that I don't know) get along? The United Nations of Salsa builds bridges, makes friends, and asks very little except that you learn the dance and have fun. While I always felt in awe of the power of salsa to connect people from different backgrounds, in recent years the bonds seem nothing short of miraculous. Salsa is the crazy glue of humanity.

In the end, my desire to dance was my body asking me to heal my mind. Salsa, which I entered into seeking nothing but joy, paid dividends in health and gave me physical stamina, body cognition, friends, community, a creative form of expression, and endorphins. Years of immersion into music and dance grounded my body, created new synapses in my brain, and allowed me to connect with my intuition. Through thousands of dances, the doubt lifted, and I trusted my instinct to follow my own beat. And that was the real lesson for me. Sometimes you have to throw up your hands and answer the calling. Even if nobody understands, least of all yourself.

Acknowledgments

This book would never have been birthed without the unwavering faith of my mother, Rafaela Castro. I can only hope that she is reading it from wherever she watches over me. Thanks to my editor, Jen O'Donnell, whose insight got me through the final push of completion. Thanks to my family for all your support, including my dad, Steve Belcher, my sister, Laura Gamboa, stepfather, John Gamboa, and many aunts, including Nina Belcher, Gillian Belcher, Judy Belcher, Elva Vallie and Linda Castro. Love and thanks to all the salsa chica angels who listened to me, read my blog, or offered up ideas. These include, Leila Decker, Jennifer Jameson, Michele Scholnick, Nobuko Kakehashi-Pavia, Julie Likht, Maria Murakawa, Lori Seamon, and Julia Lembrikova (who never let me forget about the draft she read in 2010.)

I am blessed with friends who offered up encouragement along the way. These include, Maria Bamford, for telling me to publish it even if I didn't think it was "good enough," Helen Cho, Lotus Golden, Erika Kerekes, Brian Kiley, Zena Logan, Glenn Naftchi, Alison Locke Nelson, Erin Khue Ninh, Rebecca Long, and John Sylvain.

Thanks to all my dance teachers, including Joby Brava, Christian Oviedo, Dario, and Tenia Worick.

Thank you to all my dance partners including Solomon Russell, Raul Pavia, Dong Sung An, Juan-derful, Cesar Romero, Felix Caluza, Carlos Caluza, Jhonny Gutierrez, Mark Mendez, Mike Hsiao, Charlie Antillon, Digante Saha, Dmitriy Yepishin, Tyreese Washington, Marty Herman, Eddie Hill and many more.

Utmost gratitude for my Third Street Promenade Salsa Familia for showing up every Sunday with passion and regularity, two things that don't usually go together.

Without the artists, musicians and DJ's who create and play salsa, I would have never experienced the joy of this music or had a book to write. Thank you, music, for saving my life.

And much gratitude to the energy and grace of God or the "universe" for inspiring the idea to write a book about salsa dancing and giving me the strength to finish.

About the Author

Solange Castro is a writer, comic, and actor, who was born in Berkeley, California. She attended Berkeley High School and Yale University, where she studied English literature and playwriting. Her stand-up comedy album, *A Journey of Self Discovery*, is available on iTunes, Amazon, and Spotify. She wrote and produced the play *Changes in the Mating Strategies of White People*, which ran at the Lounge Theatre in Hollywood and is now published by Broadway Play Publishing. In 2017, she directed the documentary short *A California For Everyone* about the California Environmental Quality Act's impact on the California housing crisis. When she's not writing and performing, Solange dances salsa. You can visit her website at www.solangecastro.com or read her blog, where she has been oversharing since 2003 at www.searchforsanity.com.

Bibliography

Coontz, Stephanie. *Marriage, a History*. New York: Penguin Group, 2005.

Ilich, Tijana. "What Is Salsa Music and What Is Its Origin?" ThoughtCo. Last updated August 14, 2018. https://www.thoughtco.com/the-history-of-salsa-music-2141563.

Martin, Nina. "U.S. Has The Worst Rate of Maternal Deaths In The Developed World" NPR. May 12, 2017. https://www.npr.org/2017/05/12/528098789/u-s-has-the-worst-rate-of-maternal-deaths-in-the-developed-world.

Powers, Richard. "Use It or Lose It: Dancing Makes You Smarter, Longer." Social Dance at Stanford. July 30, 2010. https://socialdance.stanford.edu/syllabi/smarter.htm.

Printed in Great Britain
by Amazon